C-3264

THIS IS YOUR **PASSBOOK**® FOR ...

SCHOOL ATTENDANCE AIDE

NATIONAL LEARNING CORPORATION®
passbooks.com

PASSBOOK® SERIES

THE *PASSBOOK® SERIES* has been created to prepare applicants and candidates for the ultimate academic battlefield – the examination room.

At some time in our lives, each and every one of us may be required to take an examination – for validation, matriculation, admission, qualification, registration, certification, or licensure.

Based on the assumption that every applicant or candidate has met the basic formal educational standards, has taken the required number of courses, and read the necessary texts, the *PASSBOOK® SERIES* furnishes the one special preparation which may assure passing with confidence, instead of failing with insecurity. Examination questions – together with answers – are furnished as the basic vehicle for study so that the mysteries of the examination and its compounding difficulties may be eliminated or diminished by a sure method.

This book is meant to help you pass your examination provided that you qualify and are serious in your objective.

The entire field is reviewed through the huge store of content information which is succinctly presented through a provocative and challenging approach – the question-and-answer method.

A climate of success is established by furnishing the correct answers at the end of each test.

You soon learn to recognize types of questions, forms of questions, and patterns of questioning. You may even begin to anticipate expected outcomes.

You perceive that many questions are repeated or adapted so that you can gain acute insights, which may enable you to score many sure points.

You learn how to confront new questions, or types of questions, and to attack them confidently and work out the correct answers.

You note objectives and emphases, and recognize pitfalls and dangers, so that you may make positive educational adjustments.

Moreover, you are kept fully informed in relation to new concepts, methods, practices, and directions in the field.

You discover that you arre actually taking the examination all the time: you are preparing for the examination by "taking" an examination, not by reading extraneous and/or supererogatory textbooks.

In short, this PASSBOOK®, used directedly, should be an important factor in helping you to pass your test.

SCHOOL ATTENDANCE AIDE

DUTIES:

The School Attendance Aide assists professional attendance personnel by contacting parents by telephone, personal visit or letter to determine the reason for student absences. Maintains an accurate record of student absences and latenesses; keeps log of absentees. Retrieves and interprets computerized student attendance information requested by guidance, attendance, administrative and teaching staffs. Prepares papers for attendance office to refer students to court; appears in court as witness. Does related work as required.

The work involves responsibility for the performance of specialized clerical and record-keeping duties associated with the monitoring of attendance of school students and the conduct of investigations into the reasons for chronic absenteeism. The work is carried out in accordance with well-established procedures and involves the collection of excuses from students; the compilation of lists of absentees; the maintenance of attendance cards; the investigation into reasons for excessive absenteeism and, where warranted, the provision of home visits and/or referrals for counseling services; and the compilation of statistics and preparation of reports as needed. Work is performed under the general supervision of the Superintendent of Schools, with wide leeway allowed the incumbent for the exercise of independent judgment in carrying out assigned duties within the established guidelines. Direct supervision is exercised over the activities of whatever subordinate clerical or paraprofessional employees may be assigned to assist the incumbent.

SCOPE OF THE EXAMINATION:

The written test will cover knowledge, skills and/or abilities in such areas as:
1. Understanding and interpreting written material;
2. Office record keeping;
3. Coding/decoding information;
4. Clerical operations with letters and numbers; and
5. Name and number checking.

HOW TO TAKE A TEST

I. YOU MUST PASS AN EXAMINATION

A. *WHAT EVERY CANDIDATE SHOULD KNOW*

Examination applicants often ask us for help in preparing for the written test. What can I study in advance? What kinds of questions will be asked? How will the test be given? How will the papers be graded?

As an applicant for a civil service examination, you may be wondering about some of these things. Our purpose here is to suggest effective methods of advance study and to describe civil service examinations.

Your chances for success on this examination can be increased if you know how to prepare. Those "pre-examination jitters" can be reduced if you know what to expect. You can even experience an adventure in good citizenship if you know why civil service exams are given.

B. *WHY ARE CIVIL SERVICE EXAMINATIONS GIVEN?*

Civil service examinations are important to you in two ways. As a citizen, you want public jobs filled by employees who know how to do their work. As a job seeker, you want a fair chance to compete for that job on an equal footing with other candidates. The best-known means of accomplishing this two-fold goal is the competitive examination.

Exams are widely publicized throughout the nation. They may be administered for jobs in federal, state, city, municipal, town or village governments or agencies.

Any citizen may apply, with some limitations, such as the age or residence of applicants. Your experience and education may be reviewed to see whether you meet the requirements for the particular examination. When these requirements exist, they are reasonable and applied consistently to all applicants. Thus, a competitive examination may cause you some uneasiness now, but it is your privilege and safeguard.

C. *HOW ARE CIVIL SERVICE EXAMS DEVELOPED?*

Examinations are carefully written by trained technicians who are specialists in the field known as "psychological measurement," in consultation with recognized authorities in the field of work that the test will cover. These experts recommend the subject matter areas or skills to be tested; only those knowledges or skills important to your success on the job are included. The most reliable books and source materials available are used as references. Together, the experts and technicians judge the difficulty level of the questions.

Test technicians know how to phrase questions so that the problem is clearly stated. Their ethics do not permit "trick" or "catch" questions. Questions may have been tried out on sample groups, or subjected to statistical analysis, to determine their usefulness.

Written tests are often used in combination with performance tests, ratings of training and experience, and oral interviews. All of these measures combine to form the best-known means of finding the right person for the right job.

II. HOW TO PASS THE WRITTEN TEST

A. *NATURE OF THE EXAMINATION*

To prepare intelligently for civil service examinations, you should know how they differ from school examinations you have taken. In school you were assigned certain definite pages to read or subjects to cover. The examination questions were quite detailed and usually emphasized memory. Civil service exams, on the other hand, try to discover your present ability to perform the duties of a position, plus your potentiality to learn these duties. In other words, a civil service exam attempts to predict how successful you will be. Questions cover such a broad area that they cannot be as minute and detailed as school exam questions.

In the public service similar kinds of work, or positions, are grouped together in one "class." This process is known as *position-classification*. All the positions in a class are paid according to the salary range for that class. One class title covers all of these positions, and they are all tested by the same examination.

B. *FOUR BASIC STEPS*

1) **Study the announcement**

How, then, can you know what subjects to study? Our best answer is: "Learn as much as possible about the class of positions for which you've applied." The exam will test the knowledge, skills and abilities needed to do the work.

Your most valuable source of information about the position you want is the official exam announcement. This announcement lists the training and experience qualifications. Check these standards and apply only if you come reasonably close to meeting them.

The brief description of the position in the examination announcement offers some clues to the subjects which will be tested. Think about the job itself. Review the duties in your mind. Can you perform them, or are there some in which you are rusty? Fill in the blank spots in your preparation.

Many jurisdictions preview the written test in the exam announcement by including a section called "Knowledge and Abilities Required," "Scope of the Examination," or some similar heading. Here you will find out specifically what fields will be tested.

2) **Review your own background**

Once you learn in general what the position is all about, and what you need to know to do the work, ask yourself which subjects you already know fairly well and which need improvement. You may wonder whether to concentrate on improving your strong areas or on building some background in your fields of weakness. When the announcement has specified "some knowledge" or "considerable knowledge," or has used adjectives like "beginning principles of…" or "advanced … methods," you can get a clue as to the number and difficulty of questions to be asked in any given field. More questions, and hence broader coverage, would be included for those subjects which are more important in the work. Now weigh your strengths and weaknesses against the job requirements and prepare accordingly.

3) Determine the level of the position

Another way to tell how intensively you should prepare is to understand the level of the job for which you are applying. Is it the entering level? In other words, is this the position in which beginners in a field of work are hired? Or is it an intermediate or advanced level? Sometimes this is indicated by such words as "Junior" or "Senior" in the class title. Other jurisdictions use Roman numerals to designate the level – Clerk I, Clerk II, for example. The word "Supervisor" sometimes appears in the title. If the level is not indicated by the title, check the description of duties. Will you be working under very close supervision, or will you have responsibility for independent decisions in this work?

4) Choose appropriate study materials

Now that you know the subjects to be examined and the relative amount of each subject to be covered, you can choose suitable study materials. For beginning level jobs, or even advanced ones, if you have a pronounced weakness in some aspect of your training, read a modern, standard textbook in that field. Be sure it is up to date and has general coverage. Such books are normally available at your library, and the librarian will be glad to help you locate one. For entry-level positions, questions of appropriate difficulty are chosen – neither highly advanced questions, nor those too simple. Such questions require careful thought but not advanced training.

If the position for which you are applying is technical or advanced, you will read more advanced, specialized material. If you are already familiar with the basic principles of your field, elementary textbooks would waste your time. Concentrate on advanced textbooks and technical periodicals. Think through the concepts and review difficult problems in your field.

These are all general sources. You can get more ideas on your own initiative, following these leads. For example, training manuals and publications of the government agency which employs workers in your field can be useful, particularly for technical and professional positions. A letter or visit to the government department involved may result in more specific study suggestions, and certainly will provide you with a more definite idea of the exact nature of the position you are seeking.

III. KINDS OF TESTS

Tests are used for purposes other than measuring knowledge and ability to perform specified duties. For some positions, it is equally important to test ability to make adjustments to new situations or to profit from training. In others, basic mental abilities not dependent on information are essential. Questions which test these things may not appear as pertinent to the duties of the position as those which test for knowledge and information. Yet they are often highly important parts of a fair examination. For very general questions, it is almost impossible to help you direct your study efforts. What we can do is to point out some of the more common of these general abilities needed in public service positions and describe some typical questions.

1) General information

Broad, general information has been found useful for predicting job success in some kinds of work. This is tested in a variety of ways, from vocabulary lists to questions about current events. Basic background in some field of work, such as sociology or economics, may be sampled in a group of questions. Often these are principles which have become familiar to most persons through exposure rather than through formal training. It is difficult to advise you how to study for these questions; being alert to the world around you is our best suggestion.

2) Verbal ability

An example of an ability needed in many positions is verbal or language ability. Verbal ability is, in brief, the ability to use and understand words. Vocabulary and grammar tests are typical measures of this ability. Reading comprehension or paragraph interpretation questions are common in many kinds of civil service tests. You are given a paragraph of written material and asked to find its central meaning.

3) Numerical ability

Number skills can be tested by the familiar arithmetic problem, by checking paired lists of numbers to see which are alike and which are different, or by interpreting charts and graphs. In the latter test, a graph may be printed in the test booklet which you are asked to use as the basis for answering questions.

4) Observation

A popular test for law-enforcement positions is the observation test. A picture is shown to you for several minutes, then taken away. Questions about the picture test your ability to observe both details and larger elements.

5) Following directions

In many positions in the public service, the employee must be able to carry out written instructions dependably and accurately. You may be given a chart with several columns, each column listing a variety of information. The questions require you to carry out directions involving the information given in the chart.

6) Skills and aptitudes

Performance tests effectively measure some manual skills and aptitudes. When the skill is one in which you are trained, such as typing or shorthand, you can practice. These tests are often very much like those given in business school or high school courses. For many of the other skills and aptitudes, however, no short-time preparation can be made. Skills and abilities natural to you or that you have developed throughout your lifetime are being tested.

Many of the general questions just described provide all the data needed to answer the questions and ask you to use your reasoning ability to find the answers. Your best preparation for these tests, as well as for tests of facts and ideas, is to be at your physical and mental best. You, no doubt, have your own methods of getting into an exam-taking mood and keeping "in shape." The next section lists some ideas on this subject.

IV. KINDS OF QUESTIONS

Only rarely is the "essay" question, which you answer in narrative form, used in civil service tests. Civil service tests are usually of the short-answer type. Full instructions for answering these questions will be given to you at the examination. But in case this is your first experience with short-answer questions and separate answer sheets, here is what you need to know:

1) Multiple-choice Questions

Most popular of the short-answer questions is the "multiple choice" or "best answer" question. It can be used, for example, to test for factual knowledge, ability to solve problems or judgment in meeting situations found at work.

A multiple-choice question is normally one of three types—

- It can begin with an incomplete statement followed by several possible endings. You are to find the one ending which *best* completes the statement, although some of the others may not be entirely wrong.
- It can also be a complete statement in the form of a question which is answered by choosing one of the statements listed.
- It can be in the form of a problem – again you select the best answer.

Here is an example of a multiple-choice question with a discussion which should give you some clues as to the method for choosing the right answer:

When an employee has a complaint about his assignment, the action which will *best* help him overcome his difficulty is to
    A. discuss his difficulty with his coworkers
    B. take the problem to the head of the organization
    C. take the problem to the person who gave him the assignment
    D. say nothing to anyone about his complaint

In answering this question, you should study each of the choices to find which is best. Consider choice "A" – Certainly an employee may discuss his complaint with fellow employees, but no change or improvement can result, and the complaint remains unresolved. Choice "B" is a poor choice since the head of the organization probably does not know what assignment you have been given, and taking your problem to him is known as "going over the head" of the supervisor. The supervisor, or person who made the assignment, is the person who can clarify it or correct any injustice. Choice "C" is, therefore, correct. To say nothing, as in choice "D," is unwise. Supervisors have and interest in knowing the problems employees are facing, and the employee is seeking a solution to his problem.

2) True/False Questions

The "true/false" or "right/wrong" form of question is sometimes used. Here a complete statement is given. Your job is to decide whether the statement is right or wrong.

SAMPLE: A roaming cell-phone call to a nearby city costs less than a non-roaming call to a distant city.

This statement is wrong, or false, since roaming calls are more expensive.
This is not a complete list of all possible question forms, although most of the others are variations of these common types. You will always get complete directions for

answering questions. Be sure you understand *how* to mark your answers – ask questions until you do.

V. RECORDING YOUR ANSWERS

Computer terminals are used more and more today for many different kinds of exams.

For an examination with very few applicants, you may be told to record your answers in the test booklet itself. Separate answer sheets are much more common. If this separate answer sheet is to be scored by machine – and this is often the case – it is highly important that you mark your answers correctly in order to get credit.

An electronic scoring machine is often used in civil service offices because of the speed with which papers can be scored. Machine-scored answer sheets must be marked with a pencil, which will be given to you. This pencil has a high graphite content which responds to the electronic scoring machine. As a matter of fact, stray dots may register as answers, so do not let your pencil rest on the answer sheet while you are pondering the correct answer. Also, if your pencil lead breaks or is otherwise defective, ask for another.

Since the answer sheet will be dropped in a slot in the scoring machine, be careful not to bend the corners or get the paper crumpled.

The answer sheet normally has five vertical columns of numbers, with 30 numbers to a column. These numbers correspond to the question numbers in your test booklet. After each number, going across the page are four or five pairs of dotted lines. These short dotted lines have small letters or numbers above them. The first two pairs may also have a "T" or "F" above the letters. This indicates that the first two pairs only are to be used if the questions are of the true-false type. If the questions are multiple choice, disregard the "T" and "F" and pay attention only to the small letters or numbers.

Answer your questions in the manner of the sample that follows:

32. The largest city in the United States is
      A. Washington, D.C.
      B. New York City
      C. Chicago
      D. Detroit
      E. San Francisco

1) Choose the answer you think is best. (New York City is the largest, so "B" is correct.)
2) Find the row of dotted lines numbered the same as the question you are answering. (Find row number 32)
3) Find the pair of dotted lines corresponding to the answer. (Find the pair of lines under the mark "B.")
4) Make a solid black mark between the dotted lines.

VI. BEFORE THE TEST

Common sense will help you find procedures to follow to get ready for an examination. Too many of us, however, overlook these sensible measures. Indeed, nervousness and fatigue have been found to be the most serious reasons why applicants fail to do their best on civil service tests. Here is a list of reminders:

- Begin your preparation early – Don't wait until the last minute to go scurrying around for books and materials or to find out what the position is all about.
- Prepare continuously – An hour a night for a week is better than an all-night cram session. This has been definitely established. What is more, a night a week for a month will return better dividends than crowding your study into a shorter period of time.
- Locate the place of the exam – You have been sent a notice telling you when and where to report for the examination. If the location is in a different town or otherwise unfamiliar to you, it would be well to inquire the best route and learn something about the building.
- Relax the night before the test – Allow your mind to rest. Do not study at all that night. Plan some mild recreation or diversion; then go to bed early and get a good night's sleep.
- Get up early enough to make a leisurely trip to the place for the test – This way unforeseen events, traffic snarls, unfamiliar buildings, etc. will not upset you.
- Dress comfortably – A written test is not a fashion show. You will be known by number and not by name, so wear something comfortable.
- Leave excess paraphernalia at home – Shopping bags and odd bundles will get in your way. You need bring only the items mentioned in the official notice you received; usually everything you need is provided. Do not bring reference books to the exam. They will only confuse those last minutes and be taken away from you when in the test room.
- Arrive somewhat ahead of time – If because of transportation schedules you must get there very early, bring a newspaper or magazine to take your mind off yourself while waiting.
- Locate the examination room – When you have found the proper room, you will be directed to the seat or part of the room where you will sit. Sometimes you are given a sheet of instructions to read while you are waiting. Do not fill out any forms until you are told to do so; just read them and be prepared.
- Relax and prepare to listen to the instructions
- If you have any physical problem that may keep you from doing your best, be sure to tell the test administrator. If you are sick or in poor health, you really cannot do your best on the exam. You can come back and take the test some other time.

VII. AT THE TEST

The day of the test is here and you have the test booklet in your hand. The temptation to get going is very strong. Caution! There is more to success than knowing the right answers. You must know how to identify your papers and understand variations in the type of short-answer question used in this particular examination. Follow these suggestions for maximum results from your efforts:

1) Cooperate with the monitor

The test administrator has a duty to create a situation in which you can be as much at ease as possible. He will give instructions, tell you when to begin, check to see that you are marking your answer sheet correctly, and so on. He is not there to guard you, although he will see that your competitors do not take unfair advantage. He wants to help you do your best.

2) Listen to all instructions

Don't jump the gun! Wait until you understand all directions. In most civil service tests you get more time than you need to answer the questions. So don't be in a hurry. Read each word of instructions until you clearly understand the meaning. Study the examples, listen to all announcements and follow directions. Ask questions if you do not understand what to do.

3) Identify your papers

Civil service exams are usually identified by number only. You will be assigned a number; you must not put your name on your test papers. Be sure to copy your number correctly. Since more than one exam may be given, copy your exact examination title.

4) Plan your time

Unless you are told that a test is a "speed" or "rate of work" test, speed itself is usually not important. Time enough to answer all the questions will be provided, but this does not mean that you have all day. An overall time limit has been set. Divide the total time (in minutes) by the number of questions to determine the approximate time you have for each question.

5) Do not linger over difficult questions

If you come across a difficult question, mark it with a paper clip (useful to have along) and come back to it when you have been through the booklet. One caution if you do this – be sure to skip a number on your answer sheet as well. Check often to be sure that you have not lost your place and that you are marking in the row numbered the same as the question you are answering.

6) Read the questions

Be sure you know what the question asks! Many capable people are unsuccessful because they failed to *read* the questions correctly.

7) Answer all questions

Unless you have been instructed that a penalty will be deducted for incorrect answers, it is better to guess than to omit a question.

8) Speed tests

It is often better NOT to guess on speed tests. It has been found that on timed tests people are tempted to spend the last few seconds before time is called in marking answers at random – without even reading them – in the hope of picking up a few extra points. To discourage this practice, the instructions may warn you that your score will be "corrected" for guessing. That is, a penalty will be applied. The incorrect answers will be deducted from the correct ones, or some other penalty formula will be used.

9) Review your answers

If you finish before time is called, go back to the questions you guessed or omitted to give them further thought. Review other answers if you have time.

10) Return your test materials

If you are ready to leave before others have finished or time is called, take ALL your materials to the monitor and leave quietly. Never take any test material with you. The monitor can discover whose papers are not complete, and taking a test booklet may be grounds for disqualification.

VIII. EXAMINATION TECHNIQUES

1) Read the general instructions carefully. These are usually printed on the first page of the exam booklet. As a rule, these instructions refer to the timing of the examination; the fact that you should not start work until the signal and must stop work at a signal, etc. If there are any *special* instructions, such as a choice of questions to be answered, make sure that you note this instruction carefully.

2) When you are ready to start work on the examination, that is as soon as the signal has been given, read the instructions to each question booklet, underline any key words or phrases, such as *least*, *best*, *outline*, *describe* and the like. In this way you will tend to answer as requested rather than discover on reviewing your paper that you *listed without describing*, that you selected the *worst* choice rather than the *best* choice, etc.

3) If the examination is of the objective or multiple-choice type – that is, each question will also give a series of possible answers: A, B, C or D, and you are called upon to select the best answer and write the letter next to that answer on your answer paper – it is advisable to start answering each question in turn. There may be anywhere from 50 to 100 such questions in the three or four hours allotted and you can see how much time would be taken if you read through all the questions before beginning to answer any. Furthermore, if you come across a question or group of questions which you know would be difficult to answer, it would undoubtedly affect your handling of all the other questions.

4) If the examination is of the essay type and contains but a few questions, it is a moot point as to whether you should read all the questions before starting to answer any one. Of course, if you are given a choice – say five out of seven and the like – then it is essential to read all the questions so you can eliminate the two that are most difficult. If, however, you are asked to answer all the questions, there may be danger in trying to answer the easiest one first because you may find that you will spend too much time on it. The best technique is to answer the first question, then proceed to the second, etc.

5) Time your answers. Before the exam begins, write down the time it started, then add the time allowed for the examination and write down the time it must be completed, then divide the time available somewhat as follows:

- If 3-1/2 hours are allowed, that would be 210 minutes. If you have 80 objective-type questions, that would be an average of 2-1/2 minutes per question. Allow yourself no more than 2 minutes per question, or a total of 160 minutes, which will permit about 50 minutes to review.
- If for the time allotment of 210 minutes there are 7 essay questions to answer, that would average about 30 minutes a question. Give yourself only 25 minutes per question so that you have about 35 minutes to review.

6) The most important instruction is to *read each question* and make sure you know what is wanted. The second most important instruction is to *time yourself properly* so that you answer every question. The third most important instruction is to *answer every question*. Guess if you have to but include something for each question. Remember that you will receive no credit for a blank and will probably receive some credit if you write something in answer to an essay question. If you guess a letter – say "B" for a multiple-choice question – you may have guessed right. If you leave a blank as an answer to a multiple-choice question, the examiners may respect your feelings but it will not add a point to your score. Some exams may penalize you for wrong answers, so in such cases *only*, you may not want to guess unless you have some basis for your answer.

7) Suggestions
   a. Objective-type questions
      1. Examine the question booklet for proper sequence of pages and questions
      2. Read all instructions carefully
      3. Skip any question which seems too difficult; return to it after all other questions have been answered
      4. Apportion your time properly; do not spend too much time on any single question or group of questions
      5. Note and underline key words – *all, most, fewest, least, best, worst, same, opposite*, etc.
      6. Pay particular attention to negatives
      7. Note unusual option, e.g., unduly long, short, complex, different or similar in content to the body of the question
      8. Observe the use of "hedging" words – *probably, may, most likely*, etc.
      9. Make sure that your answer is put next to the same number as the question
      10. Do not second-guess unless you have good reason to believe the second answer is definitely more correct
      11. Cross out original answer if you decide another answer is more accurate; do not erase until you are ready to hand your paper in
      12. Answer all questions; guess unless instructed otherwise
      13. Leave time for review

   b. Essay questions
      1. Read each question carefully
      2. Determine exactly what is wanted. Underline key words or phrases.
      3. Decide on outline or paragraph answer

4. Include many different points and elements unless asked to develop any one or two points or elements
5. Show impartiality by giving pros and cons unless directed to select one side only
6. Make and write down any assumptions you find necessary to answer the questions
7. Watch your English, grammar, punctuation and choice of words
8. Time your answers; don't crowd material

8) Answering the essay question

Most essay questions can be answered by framing the specific response around several key words or ideas. Here are a few such key words or ideas:

M's: manpower, materials, methods, money, management
P's: purpose, program, policy, plan, procedure, practice, problems, pitfalls, personnel, public relations

   a. Six basic steps in handling problems:
      1. Preliminary plan and background development
      2. Collect information, data and facts
      3. Analyze and interpret information, data and facts
      4. Analyze and develop solutions as well as make recommendations
      5. Prepare report and sell recommendations
      6. Install recommendations and follow up effectiveness

   b. Pitfalls to avoid
      1. *Taking things for granted* – A statement of the situation does not necessarily imply that each of the elements is necessarily true; for example, a complaint may be invalid and biased so that all that can be taken for granted is that a complaint has been registered
      2. *Considering only one side of a situation* – Wherever possible, indicate several alternatives and then point out the reasons you selected the best one
      3. *Failing to indicate follow up* – Whenever your answer indicates action on your part, make certain that you will take proper follow-up action to see how successful your recommendations, procedures or actions turn out to be
      4. *Taking too long in answering any single question* – Remember to time your answers properly

IX. AFTER THE TEST

Scoring procedures differ in detail among civil service jurisdictions although the general principles are the same. Whether the papers are hand-scored or graded by machine we have described, they are nearly always graded by number. That is, the person who marks the paper knows only the number – never the name – of the applicant. Not until all the papers have been graded will they be matched with names. If other tests, such as training and experience or oral interview ratings have been given, scores will be combined. Different parts of the examination usually have different weights. For example, the written test might count 60 percent of the final grade, and a rating of training and experience 40 percent. In many jurisdictions, veterans will have a certain number of points added to their grades.

After the final grade has been determined, the names are placed in grade order and an eligible list is established. There are various methods for resolving ties between those who get the same final grade – probably the most common is to place first the name of the person whose application was received first. Job offers are made from the eligible list in the order the names appear on it. You will be notified of your grade and your rank as soon as all these computations have been made. This will be done as rapidly as possible.

People who are found to meet the requirements in the announcement are called "eligibles." Their names are put on a list of eligible candidates. An eligible's chances of getting a job depend on how high he stands on this list and how fast agencies are filling jobs from the list.

When a job is to be filled from a list of eligibles, the agency asks for the names of people on the list of eligibles for that job. When the civil service commission receives this request, it sends to the agency the names of the three people highest on this list. Or, if the job to be filled has specialized requirements, the office sends the agency the names of the top three persons who meet these requirements from the general list.

The appointing officer makes a choice from among the three people whose names were sent to him. If the selected person accepts the appointment, the names of the others are put back on the list to be considered for future openings.

That is the rule in hiring from all kinds of eligible lists, whether they are for typist, carpenter, chemist, or something else. For every vacancy, the appointing officer has his choice of any one of the top three eligibles on the list. This explains why the person whose name is on top of the list sometimes does not get an appointment when some of the persons lower on the list do. If the appointing officer chooses the second or third eligible, the No. 1 eligible does not get a job at once, but stays on the list until he is appointed or the list is terminated.

X. HOW TO PASS THE INTERVIEW TEST

The examination for which you applied requires an oral interview test. You have already taken the written test and you are now being called for the interview test – the final part of the formal examination.

You may think that it is not possible to prepare for an interview test and that there are no procedures to follow during an interview. Our purpose is to point out some things you can do in advance that will help you and some good rules to follow and pitfalls to avoid while you are being interviewed.

What is an interview supposed to test?
The written examination is designed to test the technical knowledge and competence of the candidate; the oral is designed to evaluate intangible qualities, not readily measured otherwise, and to establish a list showing the relative fitness of each candidate – as measured against his competitors – for the position sought. Scoring is not on the basis of "right" and "wrong," but on a sliding scale of values ranging from "not passable" to "outstanding." As a matter of fact, it is possible to achieve a relatively low score without a single "incorrect" answer because of evident weakness in the qualities being measured.

Occasionally, an examination may consist entirely of an oral test – either an individual or a group oral. In such cases, information is sought concerning the technical knowledges and abilities of the candidate, since there has been no written examination for this purpose. More commonly, however, an oral test is used to supplement a written examination.

Who conducts interviews?

The composition of oral boards varies among different jurisdictions. In nearly all, a representative of the personnel department serves as chairman. One of the members of the board may be a representative of the department in which the candidate would work. In some cases, "outside experts" are used, and, frequently, a businessman or some other representative of the general public is asked to serve. Labor and management or other special groups may be represented. The aim is to secure the services of experts in the appropriate field.

However the board is composed, it is a good idea (and not at all improper or unethical) to ascertain in advance of the interview who the members are and what groups they represent. When you are introduced to them, you will have some idea of their backgrounds and interests, and at least you will not stutter and stammer over their names.

What should be done before the interview?

While knowledge about the board members is useful and takes some of the surprise element out of the interview, there is other preparation which is more substantive. It *is* possible to prepare for an oral interview – in several ways:

1) Keep a copy of your application and review it carefully before the interview

This may be the only document before the oral board, and the starting point of the interview. Know what education and experience you have listed there, and the sequence and dates of all of it. Sometimes the board will ask you to review the highlights of your experience for them; you should not have to hem and haw doing it.

2) Study the class specification and the examination announcement

Usually, the oral board has one or both of these to guide them. The qualities, characteristics or knowledges required by the position sought are stated in these documents. They offer valuable clues as to the nature of the oral interview. For example, if the job involves supervisory responsibilities, the announcement will usually indicate that knowledge of modern supervisory methods and the qualifications of the candidate as a supervisor will be tested. If so, you can expect such questions, frequently in the form of a hypothetical situation which you are expected to solve. NEVER go into an oral without knowledge of the duties and responsibilities of the job you seek.

3) Think through each qualification required

Try to visualize the kind of questions you would ask if you were a board member. How well could you answer them? Try especially to appraise your own knowledge and background in each area, *measured against the job sought*, and identify any areas in which you are weak. Be critical and realistic – do not flatter yourself.

4) Do some general reading in areas in which you feel you may be weak

For example, if the job involves supervision and your past experience has NOT, some general reading in supervisory methods and practices, particularly in the field of human relations, might be useful. Do NOT study agency procedures or detailed manuals. The oral board will be testing your understanding and capacity, not your memory.

5) Get a good night's sleep and watch your general health and mental attitude

You will want a clear head at the interview. Take care of a cold or any other minor ailment, and of course, no hangovers.

What should be done on the day of the interview?

Now comes the day of the interview itself. Give yourself plenty of time to get there. Plan to arrive somewhat ahead of the scheduled time, particularly if your appointment is in the fore part of the day. If a previous candidate fails to appear, the board might be ready for you a bit early. By early afternoon an oral board is almost invariably behind schedule if there are many candidates, and you may have to wait. Take along a book or magazine to read, or your application to review, but leave any extraneous material in the waiting room when you go in for your interview. In any event, relax and compose yourself.

The matter of dress is important. The board is forming impressions about you – from your experience, your manners, your attitude, and your appearance. Give your personal appearance careful attention. Dress your best, but not your flashiest. Choose conservative, appropriate clothing, and be sure it is immaculate. This is a business interview, and your appearance should indicate that you regard it as such. Besides, being well groomed and properly dressed will help boost your confidence.

Sooner or later, someone will call your name and escort you into the interview room. *This is it.* From here on you are on your own. It is too late for any more preparation. But remember, you asked for this opportunity to prove your fitness, and you are here because your request was granted.

What happens when you go in?

The usual sequence of events will be as follows: The clerk (who is often the board stenographer) will introduce you to the chairman of the oral board, who will introduce you to the other members of the board. Acknowledge the introductions before you sit down. Do not be surprised if you find a microphone facing you or a stenotypist sitting by. Oral interviews are usually recorded in the event of an appeal or other review.

Usually the chairman of the board will open the interview by reviewing the highlights of your education and work experience from your application – primarily for the benefit of the other members of the board, as well as to get the material into the record. Do not interrupt or comment unless there is an error or significant misinterpretation; if that is the case, do not hesitate. But do not quibble about insignificant matters. Also, he will usually ask you some question about your education, experience or your present job – partly to get you to start talking and to establish the interviewing "rapport." He may start the actual questioning, or turn it over to one of the other members. Frequently, each member undertakes the questioning on a particular area, one in which he is perhaps most competent, so you can expect each member to participate in the examination. Because time is limited, you may also expect some rather abrupt switches in the direction the questioning takes, so do not be upset by it. Normally, a board member will not pursue a single line of questioning unless he discovers a particular strength or weakness.

After each member has participated, the chairman will usually ask whether any member has any further questions, then will ask you if you have anything you wish to add. Unless you are expecting this question, it may floor you. Worse, it may start you off on an extended, extemporaneous speech. The board is not usually seeking more information. The question is principally to offer you a last opportunity to present further qualifications or to indicate that you have nothing to add. So, if you feel that a significant qualification or characteristic has been overlooked, it is proper to point it out in a sentence or so. Do not compliment the board on the thoroughness of their examination – they have been sketchy, and you know it. If you wish, merely say, "No thank you, I have nothing further to add." This is a point where you can "talk yourself out" of a good impression or fail to present an important bit of information. Remember, *you close the interview yourself.*

The chairman will then say, "That is all, Mr. _____, thank you." Do not be startled; the interview is over, and quicker than you think. Thank him, gather your belongings and take your leave. Save your sigh of relief for the other side of the door.

How to put your best foot forward

Throughout this entire process, you may feel that the board individually and collectively is trying to pierce your defenses, seek out your hidden weaknesses and embarrass and confuse you. Actually, this is not true. They are obliged to make an appraisal of your qualifications for the job you are seeking, and they want to see you in your best light. Remember, they must interview all candidates and a non-cooperative candidate may become a failure in spite of their best efforts to bring out his qualifications. Here are 15 suggestions that will help you:

1) Be natural – Keep your attitude confident, not cocky

If you are not confident that you can do the job, do not expect the board to be. Do not apologize for your weaknesses, try to bring out your strong points. The board is interested in a positive, not negative, presentation. Cockiness will antagonize any board member and make him wonder if you are covering up a weakness by a false show of strength.

2) Get comfortable, but don't lounge or sprawl

Sit erectly but not stiffly. A careless posture may lead the board to conclude that you are careless in other things, or at least that you are not impressed by the importance of the occasion. Either conclusion is natural, even if incorrect. Do not fuss with your clothing, a pencil or an ashtray. Your hands may occasionally be useful to emphasize a point; do not let them become a point of distraction.

3) Do not wisecrack or make small talk

This is a serious situation, and your attitude should show that you consider it as such. Further, the time of the board is limited – they do not want to waste it, and neither should you.

4) Do not exaggerate your experience or abilities

In the first place, from information in the application or other interviews and sources, the board may know more about you than you think. Secondly, you probably will not get away with it. An experienced board is rather adept at spotting such a situation, so do not take the chance.

5) If you know a board member, do not make a point of it, yet do not hide it

Certainly you are not fooling him, and probably not the other members of the board. Do not try to take advantage of your acquaintanceship – it will probably do you little good.

6) Do not dominate the interview

Let the board do that. They will give you the clues – do not assume that you have to do all the talking. Realize that the board has a number of questions to ask you, and do not try to take up all the interview time by showing off your extensive knowledge of the answer to the first one.

7) Be attentive

You only have 20 minutes or so, and you should keep your attention at its sharpest throughout. When a member is addressing a problem or question to you, give him your undivided attention. Address your reply principally to him, but do not exclude the other board members.

8) Do not interrupt

A board member may be stating a problem for you to analyze. He will ask you a question when the time comes. Let him state the problem, and wait for the question.

9) Make sure you understand the question

Do not try to answer until you are sure what the question is. If it is not clear, restate it in your own words or ask the board member to clarify it for you. However, do not haggle about minor elements.

10) Reply promptly but not hastily

A common entry on oral board rating sheets is "candidate responded readily," or "candidate hesitated in replies." Respond as promptly and quickly as you can, but do not jump to a hasty, ill-considered answer.

11) Do not be peremptory in your answers

A brief answer is proper – but do not fire your answer back. That is a losing game from your point of view. The board member can probably ask questions much faster than you can answer them.

12) Do not try to create the answer you think the board member wants

He is interested in what kind of mind you have and how it works – not in playing games. Furthermore, he can usually spot this practice and will actually grade you down on it.

13) Do not switch sides in your reply merely to agree with a board member

Frequently, a member will take a contrary position merely to draw you out and to see if you are willing and able to defend your point of view. Do not start a debate, yet do not surrender a good position. If a position is worth taking, it is worth defending.

14) Do not be afraid to admit an error in judgment if you are shown to be wrong

  The board knows that you are forced to reply without any opportunity for careful consideration. Your answer may be demonstrably wrong. If so, admit it and get on with the interview.

15) Do not dwell at length on your present job

  The opening question may relate to your present assignment. Answer the question but do not go into an extended discussion. You are being examined for a *new* job, not your present one. As a matter of fact, try to phrase ALL your answers in terms of the job for which you are being examined.

Basis of Rating

  Probably you will forget most of these "do's" and "don'ts" when you walk into the oral interview room. Even remembering them all will not ensure you a passing grade. Perhaps you did not have the qualifications in the first place. But remembering them will help you to put your best foot forward, without treading on the toes of the board members.

  Rumor and popular opinion to the contrary notwithstanding, an oral board wants you to make the best appearance possible. They know you are under pressure – but they also want to see how you respond to it as a guide to what your reaction would be under the pressures of the job you seek. They will be influenced by the degree of poise you display, the personal traits you show and the manner in which you respond.

ABOUT THIS BOOK

  This book contains tests divided into Examination Sections. Go through each test, answering every question in the margin. At the end of each test look at the answer key and check your answers. On the ones you got wrong, look at the right answer choice and learn. Do not fill in the answers first. Do not memorize the questions and answers, but understand the answer and principles involved. On your test, the questions will likely be different from the samples. Questions are changed and new ones added. If you understand these past questions you should have success with any changes that arise. Tests may consist of several types of questions. We have additional books on each subject should more study be advisable or necessary for you. Finally, the more you study, the better prepared you will be. This book is intended to be the last thing you study before you walk into the examination room. Prior study of relevant texts is also recommended. NLC publishes some of these in our Fundamental Series. Knowledge and good sense are important factors in passing your exam. Good luck also helps. So now study this Passbook, absorb the material contained within and take that knowledge into the examination. Then do your best to pass that exam.

———

EXAMINATION SECTION

EXAMINATION SECTION
TEST 1

DIRECTIONS: Each question or incomplete statement is followed by several suggested answers or completions. Select the one that BEST answers the question or completes the statement. *PRINT THE LETTER OF THE CORRECT ANSWER IN THE SPACE AT THE RIGHT.*

1. The responsibility for reporting an absentee to the bureau of attendance lies with the

    A. principal
    B. attendance coordinator
    C. official teacher
    D. school secretary

1.____

2. The agency that is responsible for the placement of a child in a foster home is the

    A. bureau of child guidance
    B. society for the prevention of cruelty to children
    C. bureau of attendance placement service
    D. department of welfare

2.____

3. When a child is paroled by the Family Court, he is placed

    A. under the direct supervision of the probation department and is to return to school at once
    B. in the custody of the parent or guardian or other adult
    C. temporarily in a children's shelter
    D. under the supervision of the attendance teacher

3.____

4. The MAJOR reason for school absence is

    A. truancy
    B. unlawful detention
    C. bussing of pupils
    D. illness

4.____

5. After making a finding of "delinquency," the judge of the school part, Family Court, places a child on probation to a probation officer and adjourns the case for 3 months. This means that

    A. the probation officer now assumes full responsibility for the child's future attendance
    B. the attendance teacher should notify the school to report all future absences to the probation officer
    C. the attendance teacher should review with the probation officer any truancies occurring during the adjourned period
    D. as soon as the child is truant again the attendance teacher should take the child back before the judge

5.____

6. A child suspended by his principal for insubordinate behavior should be   6.____

    A. taken to court by the attendance teacher on a delinquency petition
    B. excused from school until the principal decides he may be given another chance
    C. discharged from school and given an employment certificate
    D. interviewed by the assistant superintendent, who will make further determination in
        the matter

7. When a pupil is absent for any reason other than a known cause of a lawful nature, the   7.____
    principal should notify the parent or guardian on the

    A. day the absence occurs
    B. fifth day of consecutive absence
    C. third day of consecutive absence
    D. day the absence occurs only if the pupil has a poor attendance record

8. Authority to *exempt* children PERMANENTLY from attendance upon instruction is vested   8.____
    in the

    A. bureau of child guidance
    B. director of attendance
    C. superintendent of schools
    D. division of child welfare

9. A child who has been placed on the bureau of attendance medical discharge register   9.____
    may be readmitted to school ONLY

    A. if a private physician certifies that the child has recovered
    B. after examination by the school nurse
    C. at the request of the parent
    D. if the school physician reviews and approves the diagnosis and the recommenda-
        tion for return to school made by the private physician or treatment agency

10. The BASIC responsibility for the development and supervision of an effective school   10.____
    attendance program rests with the

    A. school principal
    B. district supervising attendance officer
    C. attendance coordinator
    D. attendance teacher

11. If an eligible pupil appears at a public school for admission, the principal   11.____

    A. may admit him if there is room at the pupil's grade level
    B. may refuse to admit him, pending receipt of a transfer
    C. may refuse to admit him if the school is overutilized
    D. must admit him

12. Under the domestic relations court act, one of the definitions of "delinquent child" is a 12.____
    child over 7 and under 16 years of age who

    A. is without proper guardianship
    B. deserts his home without just cause and without the consent of his parent, guard-
        ian or other custodian

2

C.   is truant from school for a week
D.   repeatedly fails to do his homework assignments

13.   The responsibility for assigning referrals to the attendance teacher lies with the   13.____

A.   attendance coordinator
B.   principal
C.   district supervising attendance officer
D.   classroom teacher

14.   Experience in the children's court has demonstrated that fining parents for their chil-   14.____
dren's failure to attend school

A.   resulted in a marked improvement in attendance
B.   did not result in a marked improvement in attendance
C.   resulted in no further court appearances
D.   improved parent-child relationships

15.   A child is deemed "neglected" under the domestic relations court act if he   15.____

A.   is habitually truant
B.   begs or solicits alms or money in public places
C.   is found in any place the maintenance of which is in violation of the law
D.   associates with immoral or vicious persons

16.   Service of a school part court summons must be made *at least*   16.____

A.   one week in advance of the hearing date
B.   5 school days in advance of the hearing date
C.   72 hours in advance of the hearing date
D.   48 hours in advance of the hearing date

17.   A child who has been placed in a hospital by order of the children's court for the purpose   17.____
of observation is considered to have been

A.   remanded
B.   committed
C.   paroled
D.   placed on probation

18.   In the enforcement of the compulsory education law, the court which has jurisdiction in   18.____
the matter of children who are over 16 years of age but not yet 18 years of age is

A.   children's court
B.   family court
C.   court of special sessions
D.   criminal court

19.   A girl 15 years of age may be legally married if she has   19.____

A.   the consent of her parents
B.   the consent of children's court
C.   the consent of the pastor of her church
D.   completed junior high school

20. A child whose parent refuses to have him vaccinated may 20.____

    A. be excused by the board of education from attending school
    B. be referred to the school part, children's court
    C. be admitted to class without vaccination if the refusal is on religious grounds
    D. obtain a medical certificate of exemption

21. The attendance teacher should make a referral to the school part, Family Court, 21.____

    A. if he is requested to do so by the class teacher
    B. after a second truancy
    C. when all other efforts to bring about the truant's adjustment have failed
    D. if the parents fail to attend a parent-child conference arranged for them

22. In exceptional cases where action is required on an emergency basis and where atten- 22.____
dance problems are minor in relation to serious delinquency, the attendance teacher
should refer cases to the

    A. bureau of adjustment, children's court
    B. division of child welfare
    C. family court
    D. district attorney

23. During several visits to the home of an absentee, the attendance teacher sees evidences 23.____
of drinking parties in which the mother is participating. He should

    A. warn that mother that she is setting a bad example
    B. file a neglect petition in school part
    C. request that the police visit the home
    D. refer the case to the society for prevention of cruelty to children

24. A mother bitterly complains that she wants her boy, aged 15, "put away," as he steals, 24.____
associates with a vicious gang, has become belligerent toward her and is a chronic truant. The attendance teacher should

    A. refer the mother to the local police precinct
    B. refer the mother to the regular part of the children's court for a petition of delin-
       quency
    C. refer the mother to a social agency
    D. process the case history for referral to the school part of the children's court

25. The continuation school law applies to 25.____

    A. minors 16 years of age who are employed part time
    B. minors 16 years of age who are employed full time
    C. the city school system only
    D. children 14 years of age employed part time

KEY (CORRECT ANSWERS)

1.	A		11.	D
2.	D		12.	B
3.	B		13.	C
4.	D		14.	B
5.	C		15.	C
6.	D		16.	D
7.	A		17.	A
8.	C		18.	A
9.	D		19.	B
10.	A		20.	B

21.	C
22.	A
23.	B
24.	D
25.	B

———

TEST 2

DIRECTIONS: Each question or incomplete statement is followed by several suggested answers or completions. Select the one that BEST answers the question or completes the statement. *PRINT THE LETTER OF THE CORRECT ANSWER IN THE SPACE AT THE RIGHT.*

1. A minor 16 years of age living in the city who desires to work as a theatrical performer must obtain an employment certificate from the   1.____

   A. mayor's office
   B. society for prevention of cruelty to children
   C. bureau of attendance
   D. license bureau

2. In carrying out the provisions of the education law, the attendance teacher is vested with the power of a   2.____

   A. peace officer
   B. parole officer
   C. warrant officer
   D. probation officer

3. A truant is a child who is   3.____

   A. a juvenile delinquent
   B. absent from school without parental knowledge
   C. frequently absent because of illness
   D. kept at home for trivial reasons by his parents

4. The person who has PRIMARY responsibility for the regular attendance of the child is the   4.____

   A. attendance teacher
   B. principal
   C. parent
   D. teacher

5. The person whose duty it is to keep the daily attendance report of a pupil is the   5.____

   A. school secretary
   B. principal
   C. guidance counselor
   D. official class teacher

6. The official or agency that determines the equivalency of the education offered to children attending non-public schools in the city is the   6.____

   A. principal of the nearest public school
   B. assistant superintendent of the district
   C. public school teacher assigned by the principal
   D. board of regents

7. The education law provides that a person   7.____

    A. over 5 and under 21 years of age is entitled to attend the public schools maintained
        in the district of his residence
    B. over 7 and under 17 years of age is entitled to attend the public schools maintained
        in the district of residence
    C. under 7 years of age registered in a public school is not yet subject to school atten-
        dance regulations
    D. over 17 years of age is entitled to attend public schools only if he is expected to
        continue until graduation

8. In the city, a child under age 7   8.____

    A. may not attend school
    B. must attend a nursery school
    C. is required by law to attend kindergarten
    D. is not required by law to attend school

9. Where a parent sends a child to school in unfit physical condition, school authorities   9.____

    A. must call the juvenile aid bureau
    B. must call the department of health
    C. may refuse the child admission
    D. may admit the child and forthwith place him on medical suspense pending further
        action

10. The compulsory education law is a   10.____

    A. federal law
    B. state law
    C. city law
    D. municipal statute

11. According to the compulsory education law, a child under 16 years of age who completes   11.____
    a four-year high school course

    A. must attend part-time school until he is 16
    B. is not required to continue his schooling
    C. must attend continuous school 20 hours per week until he is 17
    D. may go to work without an employment certificate

12. A school delinquent is a child   12.____

    A. who is habitually truant
    B. who is unlawfully employed
    C. with a court record
    D. without parental supervision

13. An attendance teacher has the power to arrest *without* warrant   13.____

    A. a parent who encourages school absence
    B. loiterers on school property
    C. any minor who is unlawfully absent from school
    D. a person illegally employing a pupil

14. In the city, a minor in proper mental and physical condition who is NOT employed must attend full-time day school from the ages of

14.____

    A. 6 to 16   B. 7 to 17   C. 7 to 16   D. 6 to 17

15. An absentee kindergarten pupil may be discharged

15.____

    A. by an attendance teacher
    B. by the principal after a period of 30 days
    C. by the principal when registration in the class is high
    D. at the request of the parent

16. An explanation which is NOT acceptable as a *lawful* reason for absence is

16.____

    A. illness in the family
    B. temporary poverty
    C. an extended vacation
    D. religious observance

17. A 17-year-old child may be discharged from school when

17.____

    A. the principal feels he is incapable of further learning
    B. he is a known truant
    C. he has been unlawfully absent for 30 consecutive days
    D. his parent requests the discharge in writing

18. When a pupil released for religious instruction is reported as an absentee from such instruction, the attendance teacher should

18.____

    A. notify the parents of the absence
    B. take no action
    C. suggest that the parents place the pupil in a parochial school
    D. notify the public school to terminate the release

19. The certificate of physical fitness required for an employment certificate is issued by

19.____

    A. a department of health physician
    B. a family physician
    C. a physician designated by the prospective employer
    D. the chairman of the health education department in the school the applicant attends

20. Attendance is NOT compulsory for the pupils in

20.____

    A. the home instruction program
    B. classes for the intellectually gifted
    C. classes for children with low IQ
    D. junior guidance classes

21. A 16-year-old child may be discharged from school to go to work when

21.____

    A. an employer signs a pledge of employment
    B. his parents so request
    C. he has received a vacation work permit
    D. he has received a standard employment certificate

22. In order to be lawfully employed, a 17-year-old boy must   22._____

    A. be a junior high school graduate
    B. attend evening high school
    C. have written permission from his parent
    D. have an employment certificate

23. The MINIMUM age at which a boy may be employed in a factory during the hours of mid-   23._____
night and 6 a.m. is

    A. 16   B. 17   C. 18   D. 19

24. A 15-year-old child who has received a special employment certificate may NOT be   24._____
employed

    A. in a factory
    B. in a mercantile establishment
    C. while school is in session
    D. until three months before his 16th birthday

25. An employed minor may be excused by the school authorities from continuation school   25._____
attendance during his employer's rush season by

    A. having a bond posted by his employer guaranteeing future school attendance
    B. reporting to school and then being permitted to leave for his place of employment
       without delay
    C. attending night school sessions during this period
    D. increasing continuation school attendance after the rush season

KEY (CORRECT ANSWERS)

1.	C	11.	B
2.	A	12.	A
3.	B	13.	C
4.	C	14.	B
5.	D	15.	D
6.	B	16.	C
7.	A	17.	D
8.	D	18.	B
9.	C	19.	A
10.	B	20.	C

21.	D
22.	D
23.	C
24.	A
25.	D

TEST 3

DIRECTIONS: Each question or incomplete statement is followed by several suggested answers or completions. Select the one that BEST answers the question or completes the statement. *PRINT THE LETTER OF THE CORRECT ANSWER IN THE SPACE AT THE RIGHT.*

1. A minor over 14 years of age may be employed WITHOUT an employment certificate as a   1.____

    A. babysitter for younger children
    B. newspaper delivery boy
    C. bootblack
    D. grocery delivery boy

2. An attendance teacher is empowered by law to enter any factory, mercantile or other establishment where a minor is believed to be employed to   2.____

    A. interview employed parents
    B. supervise cooperative education students
    C. examine employment certificates
    D. determine that employed minors receive the minimum wage

3. A boy in possession of a newspaper carrier boy certificate may NOT begin work before   3.____

    A. 5:00 a.m.   B. 6:00 a.m.   C. 7:00 a.m.   D. 8:00 a.m.

4. A married female minor who is 16-18 years of age may be *lawfully* employed   4.____

    A. without an employment certificate
    B. only with her husband's consent
    C. only at sedentary occupations
    D. only with an employment certificate

5. The number of hours that a 14-year-old minor may be permitted to work *outside* of school hours on a school day is   5.____

    A. 5   B. 2   C. 3   D. 4

6. A 15-year-old minor holding a vacation work permit may be *lawfully* employed   6.____

    A. during school hours
    B. full time during the Christmas school vacation
    C. after 6 p.m.
    D. 25 hours a week

7. A girl 16 years of age may NOT work in a restaurant between   7.____

    A. 10 p.m. and 6 a.m.   B. 8 p.m. and 6 a.m.
    C. midnight and 7 a.m.   D. 8 p.m. and midnight

8. Special employment certificates may be issued to   8.____

    A. minors 14 or 15 years of age engaged in farm work
    B. male minors 12 to 18 years of age who deliver newspapers to customers at their homes

C.   minors aged 14 and up who work as caddies after school hours
D.   minors 15 years of age found to be incapable of profiting from further instruction

9.   Evidence of age is required at the time application is made by a minor for an employment
     certificate. Of the following, the one NOT valid under the education law as proof of age is
     a(n)

     A.   affidavit of age
     B.   birth certificate
     C.   passport
     D.   transcript of birth certificate

9.____

10. When children of a family receiving public assistance are absent excessively from
     school, the attendance teacher should

     A.   refer the matter to the social investigator from the department of welfare
     B.   provide service himself on the basis of his investigation
     C.   refer the case to the society for the prevention of cruelty to children
     D.   file a petition in the children's court

10.____

11. An attendance teacher sees two truants aged 14 loitering in a candy store during school
     hours. He should

     A.   take the children's names and tell them to go to school
     B.   report the matter to the department of health
     C.   place the children in school and advise the proprietor against harboring truants
          during school hours
     D.   call the police and ask them to issue a summons to the proprietor

11.____

12. An attendance teacher observes on a visit to the home of a 6-year-old absentee that the
     mother appears emotionally disturbed during the interview. He should

     A.   notify the society for the prevention of cruelty to children of his observations con-
          cerning the mother's behavior
     B.   take no action because the child is below the compulsory school age
     C.   summon the mother to the district office immediately for a parent-child interview
     D.   clear the case with the social service exchange and interview the father and others
          to determine whether there is a threat to the health or safety of the child

12.____

13. On visiting the home of a 13-year-old girl who has been absent irregularly, the atten-
     dance teacher is informed by a 17-year-old sister that the parents are working and that
     she believes the child was sick on most of the days of her absence. The attendance
     teacher should

     A.   visit the parents after they return from work and discuss the matter with them
     B.   advise the sister of the substance of the compulsory education law
     C.   warn the child that he has reason to believe she was a truant and that her truancy
          must stop
     D.   instruct the sister to have the parents send a note to the school when the child is
          absent in the future

13.____

14. While an attendance teacher is investigating an absentee referral, his attention is directed to a 3-year-old sibling whom the mother believes to be hard of hearing. The attendance teacher should

    A. take no action as the child is under 7 years of age
    B. refer the mother to her family physician
    C. refer the mother to the school for the deaf
    D. refer the mother to the eye and ear hospital

14._____

15. An eighth-grade junior high school girl discloses to the attendance teacher that when she truants she spends her time in the home of an older girl whose parents are away at work. The attendance teacher should

    A. interview the parents of both girls to inform them of the situation
    B. serve a summons on the parents of the older girl for this unlawful assembly
    C. visit the older girl's home at the next occurrence of absence by the junior high school child
    D. warn the junior high school girl that she faces serious charges if this behavior is repeated

15._____

16. A first-year vocational high school boy who has been truanting because of his resentment over not being given the shop subject that he prefers, should FIRST be

    A. warned that he is violating the law and will be summoned to court if he continues to do so
    B. offered an interview with his guidance counselor to explore the possibility of a change in his program to enable him to obtain the desired shop subject
    C. sent to the bureau of educational and vocational guidance at headquarters for advice
    D. directed to apply at another high school for admission, accompanied by his parents

16._____

17. When the mother of a 12-year-old boy admits that she does not inform her husband of his son's truancy because he is extremely strict and punitive with the boy, the attendance teacher should

    A. warn the mother that she will have to accept sole responsibility
    B. attempt to strengthen his rapport with the boy so that he can act as a substitute father
    C. arrange to interview the boy's father to obtain his cooperation
    D. summon the mother and boy to the district office for a parent-child interview

17._____

18. The attendance teacher involved in the case of a 5-year-old kindergarten child who is exhibiting a strong fear of school should

    A. advise the mother to keep the boy at home until he is 7 years old
    B. request a medical certificate excusing the boy from attending school
    C. advise the mother to punish the boy severely if he does not attend school
    D. request the principal to refer the child to the bureau of child guidance

18._____

19. In a broken home, the child tends to

    A. become insensitive to the loss of the missing parent
    B. forget earlier experiences

19._____

C. feel ashamed, cheated and crushed
D. adapt easily to the new family relationships

20. A well-to-do parent of a 15-year-old junior high school student states that the child is doing poorly in school and wishes to go to work. The boy is well behaved, but dull and introverted. The mother hopes her son will become a lawyer.
The attendance teacher should advise her to   20._____

    A. provide psychiatric help for the boy
    B. consult with the school guidance counselor about the boy's schoolwork and his career plans
    C. accept that the boy is not college material and permit him to go to work when he is 16
    D. arrange for special tutoring so he can become a better student

21. In talking with a teacher about a child that he apprehended on the street, the attendance teacher finds that she has not recorded her class attendance for several weeks. He should then   21._____

    A. visit the teacher daily thereafter to inspect her roll book
    B. discuss the problem with his supervisor
    C. give this information to the school secretary
    D. give this information to the attendance coordinator

22. A 9-year-old truant complains that his teacher and classmates laugh at him when he is called upon in class because he doesn't "know the answers." It is BEST to   22._____

    A. consult with the classroom teacher about the problem
    B. request that the principal change the boy's class
    C. ask the guidance counselor to advise the class not to laugh at the boy
    D. advise the boy to ignore the attitude of the teacher and the class, as he must attend school

23. While an attendance teacher is in the train on his way to visit an absentee, he encounters an 11-year-old truant who states that he lives in another borough. The attendance teacher should take the   23._____

    A. child's name and tell him to go back to school
    B. child to the nearest school and ask the principal to notify the police
    C. child to the nearest police precinct and ask that the parents be notified
    D. child to his office and notify the bureau of attendance office which services the boy's school

24. When a mother of a 14-year-old junior high school boy, who has a record of truancy, informs the attendance teacher that the boy's father lives separately in a rooming house nearby, the attendance teacher should   24._____

    A. question the mother to determine whether she has notified the boy's father of his absences
    B. arrange for an interview with the boy's father and advise him that he shares parental responsibility with his wife for the boy's behavior

C.   inform the mother that she has the sole responsibility for the boy's behavior because he is living with her

D.   inform the mother that since the boy is 14 years of age he is wholly responsible for his own behavior

25.   The mother of an 11-year-old truant with an IQ of 115 tells you that he frequently quarrels with his siblings and that he complains he has nothing to do except watch television. He frequently tells untruths and sometimes steals. His school grades are poor.
The attendance teacher should tell her to

   25.____

A.   apply for help at a child guidance clinic

B.   have his father take him to ball games or to the park

C.   have the boy join the Cub Scouts

D.   give him some chores and extra homework which will keep him busy and improve his grades

---

KEY (CORRECT ANSWERS)

1.	A		11.	C
2.	C		12.	D
3.	B		13.	A
4.	D		14.	C
5.	C		15.	A
6.	B		16.	B
7.	A		17.	C
8.	D		18.	D
9.	A		19.	C
10.	B		20.	B

21.	B
22.	A
23.	D
24.	B
25.	A

TEST 4

DIRECTIONS: Each question or incomplete statement is followed by several suggested answers or completions. Select the one that BEST answers the question or completes the statement. *PRINT THE LETTER OF THE CORRECT ANSWER IN THE SPACE AT THE RIGHT.*

1. An attendance teacher finds a 12-year-old child on the street and learns that he was dis-   1._____
charged six months ago from an institution for the emotionally ill and is not yet enrolled in
any school. The attendance teacher should

    A. place the boy in the school nearest to his home and inform the school secretary
that the child must be enrolled
    B. tell the child to stay off the street and remain at home during school hours
    C. call the institution to secure from it written recommendations for the child's school-
ing
    D. issue a summons to the parent for violation of the compulsory education law

2. The BEST approach for an attendance teacher to follow in dealing with a 13-year-old   2._____
child who is a behavior problem in the classroom and a truant as well is to

    A. refer him to the principal for a warning about his misbehavior
    B. suggest that the principal have the child sit in the office for several days until he
promises to behave
    C. recommend his transfer to another class or school
    D. secure the evaluations of parents and teachers as a supplement to his own obser-
vations and discuss the case with his supervisor

3. The BEST way to help a mother who is on relief and finds it hard to manage is to   3._____

    A. suggest that she review her budget difficulties with her department of social ser-
vices investigator
    B. ask the department of social services worker to increase the budget allowances for
clothing and incidentals
    C. suggest that she review her budget difficulties with her husband
    D. ask the school PTA to help with surplus clothes and holiday gifts

4. An attendance teacher finds the parent of a chronic absentee bitter about the "bad teach-   4._____
ers" the child has. He should advise the parent to

    A. write a letter giving the facts to the local assistant superintendent
    B. write a letter giving the facts to the board of education
    C. write a letter giving the facts to the local school board
    D. visit the school and see the principal

5. An attendance teacher encounters a 12-year-old girl whom he recognizes as a child who   5._____
was discharged from school many months ago as "Not Found." He should

    A. accompany the child home, interview the parent and place the child in school
    B. obtain the child's new address from her and direct her to report to school with her
parent the following day

    C. follow the child so as to discover her new address and return in the evening to serve a summons on the parent

    D. give the child a note for admission to school and direct her to report to school immediately

6. A schoolgirl over 16 years of age who becomes pregnant out of wedlock MUST be reported to the   6._____

    A. children's court
    B. police department youth division (juvenile aid bureau)
    C. society for prevention of cruelty to children
    D. community service society

7. If the mother of a 10-year-old boy UNLAWFULLY detains him because he is allegedly unable to read, the attendance teacher should   7._____

    A. explain to her that the boy's mental capacity is probably low
    B. offer to arrange remedial work for the boy
    C. tell her that she must comply with the law immediately or face court action
    D. advise her to accompany the boy to school and discuss the problem with his teacher

8. After the birth of her baby, a 15-year-old unwed mother *may*   8._____

    A. be employed full time
    B. return to school full time
    C. attend a continuation school near her home
    D. not return to school

9. When the mother of a 13-year-old girl junior high school girl informs the attendance teacher that her daughter has returned to school, but that the child refuses to talk about her unexplained absence from home overnight, the attendance teacher should   9._____

    A. do nothing at this time, as the child has returned to school
    B. direct the mother to take her daughter to a physician for examination
    C. interview the girl at school in an effort to get at the root of the problem
    D. serve a court summons on the mother and child, as the girl is a juvenile delinquent

10. When an attendance teacher finds a 14-year-old girl who recently arrived from Puerto Rico and is not registered at any school babysitting for a 4-year-old child, he should   10._____

    A. direct the girl to report to the neighborhood school the next morning
    B. leave a summons for the parents of the 4-year-old child for unlawfully employing a 14-year-old
    C. inform the girl that she must obtain an employment certificate to continue this type of employment
    D. arrange for an interview with the parent of the girl in order to bring about her immediate admission to school

11. A 13-year-old absentee from junior high school is found at home taking care of her five younger siblings, ranging from age 2 to 10. When she informs the attendance teacher that her recently widowed mother is supporting the family by working at a store near the home, he should   11._____

A. visit the store and interview the mother so that plans can be made to enable the children to return to school without delay
B. instruct the child to inform her mother of the visit and to state that the mother is to discontinue her employment immediately, to enable the children to return to school
C. direct the oldest child to remain at home to care for the younger children but order the other children to report to school immediately
D. visit the mother's place of employment and serve her with a summons for children's court

12. A 15-year-old high school boy reveals to the attendance teacher that he is a member of a gang and that a "rumble" with lethal weapons is scheduled for that night with another neighborhood gang. The attendance teacher should   12._____

A. warn the boy of the danger of such a gang fight and suggest that he remain in the house that night
B. do nothing, as the information was given to the attendance teacher in confidence
C. warn the boy to remain away from the area of the scheduled gang fight and inform him that the attendance teacher is obligated to notify the police
D. get in touch with the parents of the boy, informing them of the scheduled gang fight affecting their son

13. After several warnings, the manager of a local theatre continues to admit minors during school hours. The attendance teacher should call this matter to the attention of the   13._____

A. local policeman on duty
B. owner of the theatre
C. youth board
D. district supervisor at the bureau of attendance

14. Experts in the field of juvenile delinquency maintain that the Glueck Prediction Scale   14._____

A. unfailingly identifies the potential truant
B. is psychologically valid
C. requires further study to validate its results
D. is a good measure because it is psychoanalytically oriented

15. The Glueck's study on "Unraveling Juvenile Delinquency" suggests that one MAJOR cause of delinquency is   15._____

A. a father who is always too strict or always too "easy"
B. an environment of constant poverty and crowded, unsanitary home conditions
C. lack of proper religious standards in the home or community
D. parents who are frequently immoral and/or who fluctuate in the way they discipline the child

16. Most of the recent evaluative studies of anti-delinquency measures indicate that   16._____

A. child guidance clinics redeem large numbers of potential delinquents in the community
B. an increase of recreational services generally decreases juvenile delinquency to a marked extent

C. reaching-out casework tends to be effective when friendly approaches to youngsters and families are persistently sustained

D. new housing projects in a slum community reduce juvenile delinquency greatly

17. Good practice requires that, whenever possible, a child who has become a delinquent should be

17.____

A. removed from possible further contamination in the community and placed in a shelter

B. treated in his own community

C. prevented from leading normal children astray by being committed for long-term treatment

D. given another opportunity to prove himself by being sent to live with relatives in another community

18. Delinquent children *most commonly* give evidence of

18.____

A. malnutrition, underweight and poor muscular coordination

B. dull-normal intelligence, deficiency in perception of spatial concepts and defective recall capabilities

C. low socio-economic background, cultural and ethical conflict

D. unhappiness and discontent with their circumstances in life

19. The *most difficult* adjustment for children going from an elementary school to a junior high school is likely to be caused by the

19.____

A. greater distance to the new school

B. increase in the number of subject teachers

C. difficulty of the new subjects

D. new children they will meet

20. A child's delinquency can *usually* be traced to

20.____

A. improper parental supervision

B. poor neighborhoods

C. a combination of many factors

D. poor schools

21. Of the following, the LEAST important basic human need is

21.____

A. affluence

B. physical well-being

C. a sense of belonging

D. recognition of one's worth

22. The redirection of undesirable interests and energies into acceptable activities is called

22.____

A. regression   B. projection
C. sublimation   D. compensation

23. The process of saving face by giving feasible but untrue excuses is called

23.____

A. repression   B. rationalization
C. fantasizing   D. compensation

24. The most *important* influence in the learning of social attitudes is the   24.____

    A. family   B. community
    C. church   D. television

25. A truant is most *often* a(n)   25.____

    A. aggressive child
    B. passive child
    C. well-adjusted child who dislikes school
    D. frustrated child

KEY (CORRECT ANSWERS)

1.	C		11.	A
2.	D		12.	C
3.	A		13.	D
4.	D		14.	C
5.	A		15.	D
6.	B		16.	C
7.	D		17.	B
8.	B		18.	D
9.	C		19.	B
10.	D		20.	C

21.	A
22.	C
23.	B
24.	A
25.	D

TEST 5

DIRECTIONS: Each question or incomplete statement is followed by several suggested answers or completions. Select the one that BEST answers the question or completes the statement. *PRINT THE LETTER OF THE CORRECT ANSWER IN THE SPACE AT THE RIGHT.*

1. The *most serious* form of emotional disturbance is labeled   1.____

    A. phobia   B. neurosis
    C. psychosis   D. anxiety

2. Of the following, the LEAST likely cause of truancy is   2.____

    A. culture conflict
    B. a broken home
    C. parental unemployment
    D. inability to read

3. The *most important* school person in the prevention of absence is the   3.____

    A. classroom teacher
    B. principal
    C. guidance counselor
    D. attendance teacher

4. To the mental hygienist, the *most serious* of the following behavior problems is   4.____

    A. cheating   B. withdrawing
    C. disobedience   D. profanity

5. A parent tells the attendance teacher that her child is exhibiting many problems. The BEST thing for the attendance teacher to do is to   5.____

    A. advise the parent to maintain strict discipline
    B. give the child an attendance card and put him on probation
    C. prepare the case for court
    D. analyze the case carefully to see what further action is warranted

6. A child may receive instruction at home from a teacher of homebound children if   6.____

    A. he is physically handicapped
    B. the parent requests this instruction
    C. the child does not like school
    D. the parent does not want him to attend a certain school

7. Proper diagnosis and treatment of the difficulties of children referred to the bureau of attendance depend MAINLY on   7.____

    A. the classroom teacher's evaluation and the child's school records
    B. the parent's statements and the home interview
    C. the completeness and accuracy of the attendance worker's findings
    D. consultation with the guidance worker

8. In using a social casework approach, the attendance teacher should   8.____

    A. direct the parent
    B. plan with the parent and child
    C. employ his authority
    D. refer the case to a family casework agency

9. School social casework goals and education goals   9.____

    A. are closely related and at times identical
    B. vary considerably according to the age level of the child
    C. are achieved through the use of the same methods
    D. are independent of each other

10. The attendance teacher's interview in the home of a truant is *most effective* when   10.____

    A. the attendance teacher clearly dominates the situation
    B. the truant is present
    C. the truant's school program is thoroughly discussed
    D. family functioning and interaction are observed

11. Of the following, the MOST important element in securing rapport with the truant is *usually*   11.____

    A. listening to his complaints about his school, family and personal life without criticism
    B. telling him he is not to blame for his behavior
    C. advising him about the correct way of getting along with others
    D. suggesting attendance at an after-school center or church activity

12. The classification of a school absence by the attendance teacher as lawful or unlawful depends on the   12.____

    A. facts presented in the case
    B. cooperation of the parents
    C. ultimate benefit to the child
    D. child's whereabouts during school hours

13. The agency which has been MOST effective in working with city gangs is   13.____

    A. Community Council
    B. Bureau of Social Service and Children's Aid Society
    C. City Youth Board
    D. Salvation Army

14. Of the following, the *eminent* authority in the field of social casework was   14.____

    A. Gordon Hamilton
    B. Henry McKenzie
    C. Robert James
    D. Louis Warren

15. The institution which cares for children suffering from grand mal is   15.____

    A. Wassaic State School
    B. Craig Colony
    C. The Children's Village, Inc.
    D. Willowbrook State School

16. An attendance teacher should refer a family to a community agency when   16.____

    A. court referral is imminent
    B. his caseload is excessively heavy
    C. specialized help is indicated
    D. the father is uncooperative

17. An attendance teacher can BEST be categorized as a   17.____

    A. pupil-personnel worker
    B. social worker
    C. probation officer
    D. guidance counselor

18. In the course of a home investigation, the attendance teacher learns that a brother of one   18.____
of his clients has developed tuberculosis of the lungs and is rapidly getting worse. The
attendance teacher should

    A. leave the house immediately
    B. counsel the family to arrange for hospital care for the sick child
    C. arrange to send the sick child to a summer camp to get well
    D. take the family to court

19. The Children's Bureau, which is part of the Federal Department of Health, Education and   19.____
Welfare, concerns itself PRIMARILY with

    A. passing child labor laws
    B. rehabilitating delinquent children
    C. improving public school programs
    D. looking after the general welfare of all children

20. Of the following, the agency which does NOT provide casework service is the   20.____

    A. Community Service Society
    B. Italian Board of Guardians
    C. Salvation Army
    D. Police Department Youth Division (Juvenile Aid Bureau)

21. If, in the course of employment with the same employer, the working hours of a minor are   21.____
changed, the employer is required to notify the

    A. bureau of attendance employment office
    B. state department of labor
    C. continuation school
    D. parents

22. An attendance teacher, upon investigation, discovers a neglect situation within a house-hold. He believes that it requires especially intensive service on the bureau's part. The case should be considered for referral to the

    A. child placement service
    B. case process program
    C. society for prevention of cruelty to children
    D. early identification program

22._____

23. A minor who is kept at home from school to assist his parents with household duties is considered to be

    A. lawfully detained   B. unlawfully detained
    C. lawfully employed   D. a truant

23._____

24. The social service exchange is a

    A. department of the Children's Bureau
    B. register for school social workers
    C. division of the department of social services
    D. service of the Community Council

24._____

25. An impoverished family cannot afford to pay for the eyeglasses that a child needs. The attendance teacher should seek the assistance of the

    A. Junior Red Cross
    B. eye and ear hospital
    C. department of correction
    D. county hospital

25._____

KEY (CORRECT ANSWERS)

1.	C		11.	A
2.	C		12.	A
3.	A		13.	C
4.	B		14.	A
5.	D		15.	B
6.	A		16.	C
7.	C		17.	A
8.	B		18.	B
9.	A		19.	D
10.	D		20.	D

21.	B
22.	B
23.	B
24.	D
25.	A

EXAMINATION SECTION
TEST 1

DIRECTIONS: Each question or incomplete statement is followed by several suggested answers or completions. Select the one that BEST answers the question or completes the statement. *PRINT THE LETTER OF THE CORRECT ANSWER IN THE SPACE AT THE RIGHT.*

Questions 1-2.

DIRECTIONS: Questions 1 and 2 are based on the following paragraph.

Screening interviews and selection interviews serve two separate and distinct purposes. Accordingly, the types of questions asked in each should tend to relate to these purposes.

1. Of the following, the question MOST appropriate for initial screening purposes generally is: 1.____

   A. What are your salary requirements?
   B. Why do you think you would like this kind of work?
   C. How did you get along with your last supervisor?
   D. What are your vocational goals?

2. Of the following, *normally* the question MOST appropriate for selection purposes generally would tend to be: 2.____

   A. Where did you work last?
   B. When did you graduate from high school?
   C. What was your average in school?
   D. Why did you select this organization?

3. When making formal business introductions between a man and a woman in official positions, the one of the following which is considered *proper* practice is, MOST generally, to present the   3.____

   A. man to the woman when the man has superior rank
   B. man to the woman when the woman has superior rank
   C. man to the woman when the woman is older but of lower rank
   D. woman to the man when their ranks are equal

4. While training a group of new student aides, an office assistant notices that one of them is not paying attention. Of the following, the MOST appropriate method for the office assistant to use in order to properly sustain attention and maintain discipline would GENERALLY be for her to   4.____

   A. reprimand the aide immediately in front of the group
   B. call a break period and then privately find out why this aide is not paying attention
   C. ask the aide to leave the training area until she has a chance to speak to him
   D. ignore the aide's behavior since the aide will be the one who will suffer later on

5. While you are working as an office assistant in the Registrar's Office, a student comes to you with a problem. Two weeks earlier, he requested that his transcript be sent to a graduate school, but at this time, it still hasn't been received by the graduate school. While speaking to you, the student becomes sarcastic and argumentative.
Of the following, it *normally* would be BEST for you to

    A. tell the student to leave the Registrar's Office and not to return for at least two days
    B. begin to treat the student in a similar manner in order to show him what his behavior is like
    C. remain calm and check to determine what has happened to the student's request
    D. treat the student politely and give him a complimentary photocopy of his transcript so that he can send it special delivery

5.____

Questions 6-15.

DIRECTIONS: Each statement in Questions 6 through 15 contains one of the faults of English usage listed below. For each, choose from the options listed the MAJOR fault contained.

OPTIONS

    A. The statement is not a complete sentence.
    B. The statement contains a word or phrase that is redundant.
    C. The statement contains a long, less commonly used word when a shorter, more direct word would be acceptable.
    D. The statement contains a colloquial expression that normally is avoided in business writing.

6. The fact that this activity will afford an opportunity to meet your group.   6.____

7. Do you think that the two groups can join together for next month's meeting?   7.____

8. This is one of the most exciting new innovations to be introduced into our college.   8.____

9. We expect to consummate the agenda before the meeting ends tomorrow at noon.   9.____

10. While this seminar room is small in size, we think we can use it.   10.____

11. Do you think you can make a modification in the date of the Budget Committee meeting?   11.____

12. We are cognizant of the problem but we think we can ameliorate the situation.   12.____

13. Shall I call you around three on the day I arrive in the city?   13.____

14. Until such time that we know precisely that the students will be present.   14.____

15. The consensus of opinion of all the members present is reported in the minutes.   15.____

Questions 16-25.

DIRECTIONS: For each of the sentences numbered 16 through 25, select from the options given below the MOST applicable choice.

OPTIONS

    A. The sentence is correct.
    B. The sentence contains a spelling error only.

C. The sentence contains an English grammar error only.
D. The sentence contains both a spelling error and an English grammar error.

16. Every person in the group is going to do his share.   16._____

17. The man who we selected is new to this University.   17._____

18. She is the older of the four secretaries on the two staffs that are to be combined.   18._____

19. The decision has to be made between him and I.   19._____

20. One of the volunteers are too young for this complecated task, don't you think?   20._____

21. I think your idea is splindid and it will improve this report considerably.   21._____

22. Do you think this is an exagerated account of the behavior you and me observed this   22._____
    morning?

23. Our supervisor has a clear idea of excelence.   23._____

24. How many occurences were verified by the observers?   24._____

25. We must complete the typing of the draft of the questionaire by noon tomorrow.   25._____

26. Which one of the following forms for the typed name of the dictator in the closing lines of   26._____
    a letter is *generally* MOST acceptable in the United States?

    A. (Dr.) James F. Fenton
    B. Dr. James F. Fenton
    C. Mr. James F. Fenton, Ph.D.
    D. James F. Fenton

27. Which of the following is MOST generally a rule to be followed when typing a rough   27._____
    draft?

    A. The copy should be single-spaced.
    B. The copy should be triple-spaced.
    C. There is no need for including footnotes.
    D. Errors must be neatly corrected.

Questions 28-30.

DIRECTIONS: Questions 28 through 30 are based on the following passage. Each paragraph
              within the passage contains one word that is incorrectly used because it is not
              in keeping with the meaning that the paragraph is evidently intended to convey.
              For each question, determine which word is incorrectly used and select from
              the choices lettered A, B, G, and D the word which, when substituted for the
              incorrectly used word, would BEST help to convey the meaning of the para-
              graph.

        *The office worker should avoid making errors in typing; but when errors are made, they
    must be unimportant. The typist should check carefully paragraph by paragraph while the
    memorandum, business form, report, or letter is in the typewriter. It is much easier to make*

corrections while the paper is in the machine. All figures, dates, and names should be checked for accuracy.

Corrections must be made on the original and on all carbon copies. If the correction is omitted only on the original and a strikeover is permitted to stand on the carbon copy, the carbon copy frequently is illegible and it is never possible to be sure after the letter has gone out that the letter itself did not contain a strikeover.

The skill of any typist may be measured by the number of errors that have been made and the way in which they have been corrected. Each error results in the loss of time and detracts from the appearance of the typed material even if it is corrected carefully. Obviously, the undesirable effects of an error are greatly reduced when the correction is made in a slovenly manner.

28. Of the following, the word which, when substituted for the incorrectly used word in the FIRST paragraph of the passage above, would BEST help to convey the meaning of the first paragraph is

    A. additions   B. corrected   C. harder   D. thoroughly

28.____

29. Of the following, the word which, when substituted for the incorrectly used word in the SECOND paragraph of the passage above, would BEST help to convey the meaning of the second paragraph is

    A. allowed   B. generally   C. made   D. remain

29.____

30. Of the following, the word which, when substituted for the incorrectly used word in the THIRD paragraph of the passage above, would BEST help to convey the meaning of the third paragraph is

    A. correction   B. increased   C. promptly   D. value

30.____

31. An office assistant needs a synonym. Of the following, the book which she would find MOST useful is

    A. a world atlas
    B. BARTLETT'S FAMILIAR QUOTATIONS
    C. a manual of style
    D. a thesaurus

31.____

32. Of the following examples of footnotes, the one that is expressed in the MOST generally accepted standard form is:
Of the following examples of footnotes, the one that is expressed in the MOST generally accepted standard form is:

    A. Johnson, T. F. (Dr.), ENGLISH FOR EVERYONE. 3rd or 4th edition: New York City Linton Publishing Company, p. 467
    B. Frank Taylor, ENGLISH FOR TODAY (New York: Rayton Publishing Company, 1971), p. 156
    C. Ralph Wilden, ENGLISH FOR TOMORROW, Reynolds Publishing Company, England, p. 451
    D. Quinn, David, YESTERDAY'S ENGLISH (New York: Baldwin Publishing Company, 1972), p. 431

32.____

33. Standard procedures are used in offices PRIMARILY because 33.____

    A. an office is a happier place if everyone is doing the tasks in the same manner
    B. particular ways of doing jobs are considered more efficient than other ways
    C. it is good discipline for workers to follow standard procedures approved by the supervisor
    D. supervisors generally don't want workers to be creative in planning their work

34. Assume that an office assistant has the responsibility of compiling, typing and distributing a preliminary announcement of Spring course offerings. The announcement will go to approximately 900 currently enrolled students. The MOST efficient method for creating and distributing this information is to 34.____

    A. type it in MS Word and send by school e-mail
    B. type it in MS Word and send by fax
    C. send it to the graphic arts department to be published and distributed as a catalog
    D. have it posted in high-traffic areas around campus

35. "Justified typing" is a term that refers MOST specifically to copy 35.____

    A. that has been edited and for which final copy is being prepared
    B. in a form that allows for an even right-hand margin
    C. with a predetermined vertical placement for each alternate line
    D. that has been approved by the supervisor and his superior

---

KEY (CORRECT ANSWERS)

1.	A	11.	C	21.	B	31.	D
2.	D	12.	C	22.	D	32.	B
3.	B	13.	D	23.	B	33.	B
4.	B	14.	A	24.	B	34.	A
5.	C	15.	B	25.	B	35.	B
6.	A	16.	A	26.	D		
7.	B	17.	C	27.	B		
8.	B	18.	C	28.	B		
9.	C	19.	C	29.	C		
10.	B	20.	D	30.	B		

TEST 2

DIRECTIONS: Each question or incomplete statement is followed by several suggested answers or completions. Select the one that BEST answers the question or completes the statement. *PRINT THE LETTER OF THE CORRECT ANSWER IN THE SPACE AT THE RIGHT.*

1. An office assistant was asked to mail a duplicated report of 100 pages to a professor in an out-of-town university. The professor sending the report dictated a short letter that he wanted to mail with the report.
    Of the following, the MOST inexpensive proper means of sending these two items would be to send the report

     1.____

    A.   and the letter first class
    B.   by parcel post and the letter separately by air mail
    C.   and the letter by parcel post
    D.   by parcel post and attach to the package an envelope with first-class postage in which is enclosed the letter

2. Plans are under way to determine the productivity of the typists who work in a central typewriting office.
    Of the procedures listed, the one generally considered the MOST accurate for finding out the typists' output is to

     2.____

    A.   keep a record of how much typing is done for specified periods of time
    B.   ask each typist how fast she types when she is doing a great deal of typewriting
    C.   give each typist a timed typewriting test during a specified period
    D.   ask the supervisor to estimate the typing speed of each subordinate.

3. Assume that an executive regularly receives the four types of mail listed below. As a general rule, his secretary should arrange his mail from top to bottom so that the top items are

     3.____

    A.   advertisements   B.   printed e-mails
    C.   business letters   D.   unopened personal letters

4. An office assistant in transcribing reports and letters from dictation should MOST generally assume that

     4.____

    A.   the transcript should be exactly what was dictated so there is little need to check any details
    B.   the dictated material is merely an idea of what the dictator wanted to say so changes should be made to improve any part of the dictation
    C.   there may be some slight changes, but essentially the transcription is to be a faithful copy of what was dictated
    D.   the transcript is merely a very rough draft and should be typed quickly so that the dictator can review it and make changes preliminary to having the final copy typed .

5. An office assistant in a city college is asked to place a call to a prospective visiting professor in Los Angeles. It is 1 P.M. in New York (EST). The time in Los Angeles is

     5.____

    A.   9 A.M.   B.   10 A.M.   C.   4 P.M.   D.   5 P.M.

6. An office assistant is given the task of creating a spreadsheet for faculty scheduling. The assistant should use which of the following software programs for this purpose?

    A. Microsoft Word
    B. Adobe Acrobat Pro
    C. Microsoft Excel
    D. MyFacultyScheduling iPhone app

6.____

7. An office assistant is in the process of typing the forms for recommendation for promotion for a member of the faculty who is away for a week. She notes that two books of which he is the author are listed without dates.
Of the following, the procedure she should BEST follow at this point *generally,* is to

    A. postpone doing the job until the professor returns to campus the following week
    B. type the material omitting the books
    C. check the professor's office for copies of the books and obtain the correct data
    D. call the professor's wife and ask her when the books were published.

7.____

8. An office has introduced work standards for all the employees. Of the following, it is MOST likely that use of such standards would tend to

    A. make it more difficult to determine numbers of employees needed
    B. lead to a substantial drop in morale among all of the employees
    C. reduce the possibility of planning to meet emergencies
    D. reduce uncertainty about the costs of doing tasks

8.____

9. In preparing a report that includes several tables, if not otherwise instructed, the typist should MOST properly include a list of tables

    A. in the introductory part of the report
    B. at the end of each chapter in the body of the report
    C. in the supplementary part of the report as an appendix
    D. in the supplementary part of the report as a part of the index

9.____

10. Assume that a dictator is briefly interrupted because of a telephone call or other similar matter (no more than three minutes).
Of the following tasks, the person taking the dictation should NORMALLY use the time to

    A. re-read notes already recorded
    B. tidy the dictator's desk
    C. check the accuracy of the dictator's desk files
    D. return to her own desk to type the dictated material

10.____

11. The chairman of an academic department tells an office assistant that a meeting of the faculty is to be held four weeks from the current date.
Of the following responsibilities, the office assistant is MOST frequently held responsible for

    A. planning the agenda of the meeting
    B. presiding over the conduct of the meeting
    C. reserving the meeting room and notifying the members
    D. initiating all formal resolutions.

11.____

12. For the office assistant whose duties include frequent recording and transcription of minutes of formal meetings, the one of the following reference works *generally* considered to be MOST useful is: 12.____

    A. Robert's RULES OF ORDER
    B. Bartlett's FAMILIAR QUOTATIONS
    C. WORLD ALMANAC AND BOOK OF FACTS
    D. Conway's REFERENCE

13. Of the following statements about the numeric system of filing, the one which is CORRECT is that it   13.____

    A. is the least accurate of all methods of filing
    B. eliminates the need for cross-referencing
    C. allows for very limited expansion
    D. requires a separate index

14. When more than one name or subject is involved in a piece of correspondence to be filed, the office assistant should *generally*   14.____

    A. prepare a cross-reference sheet
    B. establish a geographical filing system
    C. prepare out-guides
    D. establish a separate index card file for noting such correspondence

15. A tickler file is MOST generally used for   15.____

    A. identification of material contained in a numeric file
    B. maintenance of a current listing of telephone numbers
    C. follow-up of matters requiring future attention
    D. control of records borrowed or otherwise removed from the files

16. In filing, the name Ms. "Ann Catalana-Moss" should *generally* be indexed as   16.____

    A. Moss, Catalana, Ann (Ms.)
    B. Catalana-Moss, Ann (Ms.)
    C. Ann Catalana-Moss (Ms.)
    D. Moss-Catalana, Ann (Ms.)

17. An office assistant has a set of four cards, each of which contains one of the following names.   17.____
In alphabetic filing, the FIRST of the cards to be filed is

    A. Ms. Alma John
    B. Mrs. John (Patricia) Edwards
    C. John-Edward School Supplies, Inc.
    D. John H. Edwards

18. Generally, of the following, the name to be filed FIRST in an alphabetical filing system is   18.____

    A. Diane Maestro   B. Diana McElroy
    C. James Mackell   D. James McKell

19. According to generally recognized rules of filing in an alphabetic filing system, the one of   19.____
the following names which *normally* should be filed LAST is

    A. Department of Education, New York State
    B. F. B. I.
    C. Police Department of New York City
    D. P. S. 81 of New York City

Questions 20-21.

DIRECTIONS: Answer Questions 20 and 21 SOLELY on the basis of the information provided in the following passage.

Auto: *Auto travel requires prior approval by the President and/or appropriate Dean and must be indicated in the "Request for Travel Authorization" form. Employees authorised to use personal autos on official college business will be reimbursed at the rate of 14¢ per mile for the first 500 miles driven and 9¢ per mile for mileage driven in excess of 500 miles. The Comptroller's Office of the City of New York may limit the amount of reimbursement to the expenditure that would have been made if a less expensive mode of transportation (railroad, airplane, bus, etc.) had been utilized. If this occurs, the traveler will have to pick up the excess expenditure as a personal expense.*

Tolls, Parking Fees and Parking Meter Fees are not reimbursable, and may NOT be claimed.

20. Suppose that Professor T. gives the office assistant the following memorandum: 20.____
    Used car for official trip to Albany, New York, and return. Distance from New York to Albany is 148 miles.
    Tolls were $1.75 each way. Parking garage cost $1.50.
    When preparing the Travel Expense Voucher for Professor T., the figure which should be claimed for transportation is

    A. $60.44   B. $56.94   C. $41.44   D. $25.72

21. Suppose that Professor V. gives the office assistant the following memorandum: 21.____
    Used car for official trip to Pittsburgh, Pennsylvania, and return. Distance from New York to Pittsburgh is 350 miles. Tolls were $1.65, $5.70 going, and $1.65, $1.00 returning.
    When preparing the Travel Expense Voucher for Professor V., the figure which should be claimed for transportation is

    A. $112.70   B. $88.00   C. $63.70   D. $49.00

Questions 22-23.

DIRECTIONS: Answer Questions 22 and 23 SOLELY on the basis of the following summary of salary increases applicable to a group of exempt student interns.

Hourly Rate - 6/30/14	Increase - 7/1/14	Increase - 7/1/15
$10.20	$1.40/hr	$1.40/hr
11.20	1.20/hr	1.20/hr
12.20	1.20/hr	1.20/hr
13.20	1.00/hr	1.00/hr
14.20	1.00/hr	1.00/hr
15.20	1.00/hr	1.00/hr

22. A college office employee with an hourly salary of $14.20 as of June 30, 2014 worked for 22.____
32 hours during the week of April 16, 2015. Her GROSS salary for that week was

   A. $422.40   B. $454.40   C. $486.40   D. $518.40

23. A college office employee was earning an hourly salary of $12.20 in June of 2014. The 23.____
percentage increase in her hourly salary as of July 2, 2015 will be *most nearly* _____
percent.

   A. 10   B. 15   C. 20   D. 25

Questions 24-25.

DIRECTIONS: Answer Questions 24 and 25 SOLELY on the basis of the information con-
              tained in the following chart.

ENROLLMENT ACCORDING TO DEPARTMENTAL MAJOR

1273 4273

MAJOR	Borough of Manhattan Community DAY	EVE	Bronx Community DAY	EVE	Hostos Comm. DAY	EVE	Kingsboro Community DAY	EVE	LaGuardia Community DAY	EVE	N.Y.C. Community Bklyn. Center DAY	Voorhess Center DAY	Queensboro Community DAY	EVE
Accounting *	1202	4202	0802	3802			1002	4002	(1802)	(4802)	1302	1702	0902	3902
Advertising *														
Afro-American Studies *			0837	3837							1337			
Bio-Med. Computer Sciences *														
Black Studies *											1337			
Business Administration *	1208	4208	0808	3808			1008	4008	(1808)	(4808)			0908	3908
Business Education *	1213	4213	0813	3813										
Business Management *	*1273	4273							(1841)	(4841)			0941	3941
Chemical Technology *											1316			
Chemistry *			0837	3837			1039	4039			1337			
Child Care *					(1483)		1083				(1383)	1783		
Chinese														

CIRCLED SESSION CODES: THESE PROGRAMS DO NOT ADMIT NEW STUDENTS IN FEBRUARY
*COMMUNITY COLLEGE PROGRAMS WHICH ARE TRANSFERABLE TO RELATED SENIOR COLLEGE PROGRAMS

24. Suppose that a student talks with the office assistant in December about admission to a program in Business Administration as soon as possible. From the information provided in the above chart, _____ community colleges have day programs in Business Administration that begin at mid-year.

   24.____

    A. Two   B. Four   C. Five   D. Six

25. Of the following majors, which one may NOT be studied during the evening at any of the community colleges shown in the above chart?

   25.____

    A. Afro-American Studies   B. Business Education
    C. Chemistry   D. Child Care

Questions 26-27.

DIRECTIONS: Answer Questions 26 and 27 SOLELY on the basis of the information contained in the following table.

Comparison of CUNY Attrition Rates for Fall 2015 Day Freshmen through Fall 2016

Colleges	Open Admissions (a)	Regular (b)	Overall
Senior	30%	14%	21%
Community	40%	34%	39%
Total	36%	20%	29%

   (a) Represents senior college students admitted with high school averages below 80 and community college students admitted with high school averages below 75.
   (b) Represents senior college students admitted with averages of 80 and above and community college students admitted with averages of 75 and above.

26. The category of students who remained in the City University in the GREATEST proportion were

   26.____

    A. regular students in community colleges
    B. open admissions students in community colleges
    C. regular students in senior colleges
    D. open admissions students in senior colleges

27. REGULAR admission to a senior college was on the basis of an academic average

   27.____

    A. above 70   B. of 80 or above
    C. above 75   D. above 85

Questions 28-30.

DIRECTIONS: Answer Questions 28 through 30 SOLELY on the basis of the information contained in the passage below.

Hereafter, all SEEK students interested in transferring to community college career programs (associate degrees) from liberal arts programs in senior colleges (bachelor degrees) will be eligible for such transfers if they have completed no more than three semesters.

For students with averages of 1.5 or above, transfer will be automatic. Those with 1.0 to 1.5 averages can transfer provisionally and will be required to make substantial progress during the first semester in the career program. Once transfer has taken place, only those courses in which passing grades were received will be computed in the community college gradepoint average.

No request for transfer will be accepted from SEEK students wishing to enter the liberal arts programs at the community college.

28. According to this passage, the one of the following which is the BEST statement concerning the transfer of SEEK students is that a SEEK student   28.____

    A. may transfer to a career program at the end of one semester
    B. must complete three semester hours before he is eligible for transfer
    C. is not eligible to transfer to a career program
    D. is eligible to transfer to a liberal arts program

29. Which of the following is the BEST statement of academic evaluation for transfer purposes in the case of SEEK students?   29.____

    A. No SEEK student with an average under 1.5 may transfer.
    B. A SEEK student with an average of 1.3 may not transfer.
    C. A SEEK student with an average of 1.6 may transfer.
    D. A SEEK student with an average of .8 may transfer on a provisional basis.

30. It is MOST likely that, of the following, the NEXT degree sought by one who already holds the Associate in Science degree would be a(n)   30.____

    A. Assistantship in Science degree
    B. Associate in Applied Science degree
    C. Bachelor of Science degree
    D. Doctor of Philosophy degree

KEY (CORRECT ANSWERS)

1.	D	11.	C	21.	B
2.	A	12.	A	22.	C
3.	D	13.	D	23.	C
4.	C	14.	A	24.	B
5.	B	15.	C	25.	D
6.	C	16.	B	26.	C
7.	C	17.	D	27.	B
8.	D	18.	C	28.	A
9.	A	19.	B	29.	C
10.	A	20.	C	30.	C

EXAMINATION SECTION
TEST 1

DIRECTIONS: Each question or incomplete statement is followed by several suggested answers or completions. Select the one that BEST answers the question or completes the statement. *PRINT THE LETTER OF THE CORRECT ANSWER IN THE SPACE AT THE RIGHT.*

Questions 1-6.

DIRECTIONS: Questions 1 through 6 each consist of four sentences. Choose the one sentence in each set of four that would be BEST for a formal letter or report. Consider grammar and appropriate usage.

1. A. These statements can be depended on, for their truth has been guaranteed by reliable city employees.
    B. Reliable city employees guarantee the facts with regards to the truth of these statements.
    C. Most all these statements have been supported by city employees who are reliable and can be depended upon.
    D. The city employees which have guaranteed these statements are reliable.

1.____

2. A. I believe the letter was addressed to either my associate or I.
    B. If properly addressed, the letter will reach my associate and I.
    C. My associate's name, as well as mine, was on the letter.
    D. The letter had been addressed to myself and my associate.

2.____

3. A. The secretary would have corrected the errors if she knew that the supervisor would see the report.
    B. The supervisor reprimanded the secretary, whom she believed had made careless errors.
    C. Many errors were found in the report which she typed and could not disregard them.
    D. The errors in the typed report were so numerous that they could hardly be overlooked.

3.____

4. A. His consultant was as pleased as he with the success of the project.
    B. The success of the project pleased both his consultant and he.
    C. he and also his consultant was pleased with the success of the project.
    D. Both his consultant and he was pleased with the success of the project.

4.____

5. A. Since the letter did not contain the needed information, it was not real useful to him.
    B. Being that the letter lacked the needed information, he could not use it.
    C. Since the letter lacked the needed information, it was of no use to him.
    D. This letter was useless to him because there was no needed information in it.

5.____

6.   A.   Scarcely had the real estate tax increase been declared than the notices were   6.____
            sent out.
      B.   They had no sooner declared the real estate tax increases when they sent the
            notices to the owners.
      C.   The city had hardly declared the real estate tax increase till the notices were pre-
            pared for mailing.
      D.   No sooner had the real estate tax increase been declared than the notices were
            sent out.

Questions 7-14.

DIRECTIONS: Answer Questions 7 through 14 on the basis of the following passage.

      Important figures in education and in public affairs have recommended development of a
private organization sponsored in part by various private foundations which would offer
installment payment plans to full-time matriculated students in accredited colleges and uni-
versities in the United States and Canada. Contracts would be drawn to cover either tuition
and fees, or tuition, fees, room and board in college facilities, from one year up to and including six years. A special charge, which would vary with the length of the contract, would be
added to the gross repayable amount. This would be in addition to interest at a rate which
would vary with the income of the parents. There would be a 3% annual interest charge for
families with total income, before income taxes of $10,000 or less. The rate would increase by
1/10 of 1% for every $200 of additional net income in excess of $10,000 up to a maximum of
10% interest. Contracts would carry an insurance provision on the life of the parent or guardian who signs the contract; all contracts must have the signature of a parent or guardian. Payment would be scheduled in equal monthly installments.

7.   Which of the following students would be eligible for the payment plan described in the   7.____
      above passage?
      A

      A.   matriculated student taking 6 semester hours toward a graduate degree at CCNY
      B.   matriculated student taking 17 semester hours toward an undergraduate degree at
            Brooklyn College
      C.   CCNY graduate matriculated at the University of Mexico, taking 18 semester hours
            toward a graduate degree
      D.   student taking 18 semester hours in a special pre-matriculation program at Hunter
            College

8.   According to the above passage, the organization described would be sponsored in part   8.____
      by

      A.   private foundations
      B.   colleges and universities
      C.   persons in the field of education
      D.   persons in public life

9.   Which of the following expenses could NOT be covered by a contract with the organiza-   9.____
      tion described in the above passage?

      A.   Tuition amounting to $4,000 per year
      B.   Registration and laboratory fees

    C. Meals at restaurants near the college
    D. Rent for an apartment in a college dormitory

10. The total amount to be paid would include ONLY the   10._____

    A. principal
    B. principal and interest
    C. principal, interest, and special charge
    D. principal, interest, special charge, and fee

11. The contract would carry insurance on the   11._____

    A. life of the student
    B. life of the student's parents
    C. income of the parents of the student
    D. life of the parent who signed the contract

12. The interest rate for an annual loan of $5,000 from the organization described in the pas- 12._____
    sage for a student whose family's net income was $11,000 should be

    A. 3%   B. 3.5%   C. 4%   D. 4.5%

13. The interest rate for an annual loan of $7,000 from the organization described in the pas- 13._____
    sage for a student whose family's net income was $20,000 should be

    A. 5%   B. 8%   C. 9%   D. 10%

14. John Lee has submitted an application for the installment payment plan described in the 14._____
    passage. John's mother and father have a store which grossed $100,000 last year, but
    the income which the family received from the store was $18,000 before taxes. They also
    had $1,000 income from stock dividends. They paid $2,000 in income taxes.
    The amount of income upon which the interest should be based is

    A. $17,000   B. $18,000   C. $19,000   D. $21,000

15. One of the MOST important techniques for conducting good interviews is   15._____

    A. asking the applicant questions in rapid succession, thereby keeping the conversa-
        tion properly focused
    B. listening carefully to all that the applicant has to say, making mental notes of possi-
        ble areas for follow-up
    C. indicating to the applicant the criteria and standards on which you will base your
        judgment
    D. making sure that you are interrupted above five minutes before you wish to end so
        that you can keep on schedule

16. You are planning to conduct preliminary interviews of applicants for an important position 16._____
    in your department. Which of the following planning considerations is LEAST likely to
    contribute to successful interviews?

    A. Make provisions to conduct interviews in privacy
    B. Schedule your appointments so that interviews will be short
    C. Prepare a list of your objectives
    D. Learn as much as you can about the applicant before the interview.

17. In interviewing job applicants, which of the following usually does NOT have to be done   17.____
    before the end of the interview?

    A. Making a decision to hire an applicant
    B. Securing information from applicants
    C. Giving information to applicants
    D. Establishing a friendly relationship with applicants

18. In the process of interviewing applicants for a position on your staff, the one of the follow-   18.____
    ing which would be BEST is to

    A. make sure all applicants are introduced to the other members of your staff prior to
       the formal interview
    B. make sure the applicant does not ask questions about the job or the department
    C. avoid having the applicant talk with the staff under any circumstances
    D. introduce applicants to some of the staff at the conclusion of a successful interview

19. While interviewing a job applicant, you ask why the applicant left his last job. The appli-   19.____
    cant does not answer immediately.
    Of the following, the BEST action to take at that point is to

    A. wait until he answers
    B. ask another question
    C. repeat the question in a loud voice
    D. ask him why he does not answer

20. Which of the following actions would be LEAST desirable for you to take when you have   20.____
    to conduct an interview?

    A. Set a relaxed and friendly atmosphere
    B. Plan your interview ahead of time
    C. Allow the person interviewed to structure the interview as he wishes
    D. Include some stock or standard question which you ask everyone

21. You know that a student applying for a job in your office has done well in college except   21.____
    for two courses in science. However, when you ask him about his grades, his reply is
    vague and general.
    It would be BEST for you to

    A. lead the applicant to admitting doing poorly in science to be sure that the facts are
       correct
    B. judge the applicant's tact and skill in handling what may be for him a personally
       sensitive question
    C. immediately confront the applicant with the facts and ask for an explanation
    D. ignore the applicant's response since you have the transcript

22. A college student has applied for a position with your department. Prior to conducting an   22.____
    interview of the job applicant, it would be LEAST helpful for you to have

    A. a personal resume   B. a job description
    C. references   D. hiring requirements

23. Job applicants tend to be nervous during interviews. Which of the following techniques is MOST likely to put such an applicant at ease?   23._____

    A. Try to establish rapport by asking general questions which are easily answered by the applicant
    B. Ask the applicant to describe his career objectives immediately, thus minimizing the anxiety caused by waiting
    C. Start the interview with another member of the staff present so that the applicant does not feel alone
    D. Proceed as rapidly as possible, since the emotional state of the applicant is none of your concern

24. Of the following abilities, the one which is LEAST important in conducting an interview is the ability to   24._____

    A. ask the interviewee pertinent questions
    B. evaluate the interviewee on the basis of appearance
    C. evaluate the responses of the interviewee
    D. gain the cooperation of the interviewee

25. One of the techniques of management often used by supervisors is performance appraisal.   25._____
Which of the following is NOT one of the objectives of performance appraisal?

    A. Improve staff performance
    B. Determine individual training needs
    C. Improve organizational structure
    D. Set standards and performance criteria for employees

KEY (CORRECT ANSWERS)

1.	A		11.	D
2.	C		12.	B
3.	D		13.	B
4.	A		14.	C
5.	C		15.	B
6.	D		16.	B
7.	B		17.	A
8.	A		18.	D
9.	C		19.	A
10.	C		20.	C

21. B
22. C
23. A
24. B
25. C

TEST 2

DIRECTIONS: Each question or incomplete statement is followed by several suggested answers or completions. Select the one that BEST answers the question or completes the statement. *PRINT THE LETTER OF THE CORRECT ANSWER IN THE SPACE AT THE RIGHT.*

1. Examine the following sentence, and then choose the BEST statement about it from the choices below.   1.____
   Clerks are expected to receive visitors, to answer telephones, and miscellaneous clerical work must be done.

   A. This sentence is an example of effective writing.
   B. This is a *run-on* sentence.
   C. The three ideas in this sentence are not parallel, and therefore they should be divided into separate sentences.
   D. The three ideas in this sentence are parallel, but they are not expressed in parallel form.

2. Examine the following sentence, and then choose from below the word which should be inserted in the blank space.   2.____
   Mr. Luce is a top-notch interviewer, _____ he is very reliable.

   A. but   B. and   C. however   D. for

3. Examine the following sentence, and then choose from below the words which should be inserted in the blank spaces.   3.____
   The committee _____ sent in _____ report.

   A. has; it's   B. has; their
   C. have; its   D. has; its

4. Examine the following sentence, and then choose from below the words which should be inserted in the blank spaces.   4.____
   An organization usually contains more than just a few people; usually the membership is _____ enough so that close personal relationships among _____ impossible.

   A. large; are   B. large; found
   C. small; becomes   D. small; is

5. Of the following, the BEST reference book to use to find a synonym for a common word is a(n)   5.____

   A. thesaurus   B. dictionary
   C. encyclopedia   D. catalog

Questions 6-10.

DIRECTIONS: Questions 6 through 10 concern college students who have just completed their junior year for whom you must calculate grade averages for the year. These averages are to be based on the following table showing the number of credit hours for each student during the year at each of the grade levels: A, B, C, D, and F. How these letter grades may be translated into numerical grades is indicated in the first column of the table.

Grade Value	Credit Hours- Junior Year					
	King	Lewis	Martin	Nonkin	Ottly	Perry
A = 95	12	6	15	3	9	-
B = 85	9	15	6	12	9	3
C = 75	6	9	9	12	3	27
D = 65	3	-	3	3	6	-
F = 0	-	-	-	3	-	-

Calculating a grade average for an individual student is a 4-step process:

I. Multiply each grade value by the number of credit hours for which the student received that grade
II. Add these multiplication products for each student
III. Add the student's total credit hours
IV. Divide the multiplication product total by the total number of credit hours
V. Round the result, if there is a decimal place, to the nearest whole number. A number ending in .5 would be rounded to the next higher number

<u>Example</u>

Using student King's grades as an example, his grade average can be calculated by going through the following four steps:

I.
95 x 12 = 1140
85 x 9 = 765
75 x 6 = 450
65 x 3 = 195
0 x 0 = 0

III.
12
9
6
3
0
30 TOTAL credit hours

II. Total = 2550

IV. Divide 2550 by 30: $\dfrac{2550}{30} = 85$

King's grade average is 85.

Answer Questions 6 through 10 on the basis of the information given above.

6. The grade average of Lewis is

   A. 83   B. 84   C. 85   D. 86

   6.____

7. The grade average of Martin is

   A. 83   B. 84   C. 85   D. 86

   7.____

8. The grade average of Nonkin is

   A. 72   B. 73   C. 79   D. 80

   8.____

9. Student Ottly must attain a grade average of 85 in each of his years in college to be accepted into graduate school.
   If, in summer school during his junior year, he takes two 3-credit courses and receives a grade of 85 in one and 95 in the other, his grade average for his junior year will then be MOST NEARLY

   A. 82   B. 83   C. 84   D. 85

   9.____

10. If Perry takes an additional 3-credit course during the year and receives a grade of 95, his grade average will be increased to approximately   10._____

    A. 74   B. 76   C. 78   D. 80

11. You are in charge of verifying employees' qualifications. This involves telephoning previous employers and schools. One of the applications which you are reviewing contains information which you are almost certain is correct on the basis of what the employee has told you.
The BEST thing to do is to   11._____

    A. check the information again with the employee
    B. perform the required verification procedures
    C. accept the information as valid
    D. ask a superior to verify the information

12. The practice of immediately identifying oneself and one's place of employment when contacting persons on the telephone is   12._____

    A. *good,* because the receiver of the call can quickly identify the caller and establish a frame of reference
    B. *good,* because it helps to set the caller at ease with the other party
    C. *poor,* because it is not necessary to divulge that information when making general calls
    D. *poor,* because it takes longer to arrive at the topic to be discussed

13. A supervisor, Miss Smith, meets with a group of subordinates and tells them how they should perform certain tasks. The meeting is highly successful. She then attends a meeting to discuss common problems with a group of fellow supervisors with duties similar to her own. When she tells them how their subordinates should perform the same tasks, some of the other supervisors become angry.
Of the following, the MOST likely reason for this anger is that   13._____

    A. tension is to be expected in situations in which supervisors deal with each other
    B. the other supervisors are jealous of Miss Smith's knowledge
    C. Miss Smith should not tell other supervisors what methods she uses
    D. Miss Smith does not correctly perceive her role in relation to other supervisors

14. There is considerable rivalry among employees in a certain department over location of desks. It is the practice of the supervisor to assign desks without any predetermined plan. The supervisor is reconsidering his procedure.
In assigning desks, PRIMARY consideration should ordinarily be given to   14._____

    A. past practices
    B. flow of work
    C. employee seniority
    D. social relations among employees

15. Assume that, when you tell some of the typists under your supervision that the letters they prepare have too many errors, they contend that the letters are readable and that they obtain more satisfaction from their jobs if they do not have to be as concerned about errors.
These typists are

15.____

    A. *correct,* because the ultimate objective should be job satisfaction
    B. *incorrect,* because every job should be performed perfectly
    C. *correct,* because they do not compose the letters themselves
    D. *incorrect,* because their satisfaction is not the only consideration

16. Which of the following possible conditions is LEAST likely to represent a hindrance to effective communication?

16.____

    A. The importance of a situation may not be apparent.
    B. Words may mean different things to different people.
    C. The recipient of a communication may respond to it, sometimes unfavorably.
    D. Communications may affect the self-interest of those communicating.

17. You are revising the way in which your unit handles records.
One of the BEST ways to make sure that the change will be implemented with a minimum of difficulty is to

17.____

    A. allow everyone on the staff who is affected by the change to have an opportunity to contribute their ideas to the new procedures
    B. advise only the key members of your staff in advance so that they can help you enforce the new method when it is implemented
    C. give the assignment of implementation to the newest member of the unit
    D. issue a memorandum announcing the change and stating that complaints will not be tolerated

18. One of your assistants is quite obviously having personal problems that are affecting his work performance.
As a supervisor, it would be MOST appropriate for you to

18.____

    A. avoid any inquiry into the nature of the situation since this is not one of your responsibilities
    B. avoid any discussion of personal problems on the basis that there is nothing you could do about them anyhow
    C. help the employee obtain appropriate help with these problems
    D. advise the employee that personal problems cannot be considered when evaluating work performance

19. The key to improving communication with your staff and other departments is the development of an awareness of the importance of communication.
Which of the following is NOT a good suggestion for developing this awareness?

19.____

    A. Be willing to look at your own attitude toward how you communicate.
    B. Be sensitive and receptive to reactions to what you tell people.
    C. Make sure all communication is in writing.
    D. When giving your subordinates directions, try to put yourself in their place and see if your instructions still make sense.

20. One of the assistants on your staff has neglected to complete an important assignment 20.____
on schedule. You feel that a reprimand is necessary.
When speaking to the employee, it would usually be LEAST desirable to

    A. display your anger to show the employee how strongly you feel about the problem
    B. ask several questions about the reasons for failure to complete the assignment
    C. take the employee aside so that nobody else is present when you discuss the matter
    D. give the employee as much time as he needs to explain exactly what happened

_____

KEY (CORRECT ANSWERS)

1.	D	11.	B
2.	B	12.	A
3.	D	13.	D
4.	A	14.	B
5.	A	15.	D
6.	B	16.	C
7.	C	17.	A
8.	B	18.	C
9.	C	19.	C
10.	C	20.	A

_____

EXAMINATION SECTION
TEST 1

DIRECTIONS: Each question or incomplete statement is followed by several suggested
answers or completions. Select the one that BEST answers the question or
completes the statement. *PRINT THE LETTER OF THE CORRECT ANSWER
IN THE SPACE AT THE RIGHT.*

1. One of the things that can ruin morale in a work group is the failure to exercise judgment   1.____
in the assignment of overtime work to your subordinates.
Of the following, the MOST desirable supervisory practice in assigning overtime work
is to

    A. *rotate* overtime on a uniform basis among all your subordinates
    B. *assign* overtime to those who are *moonlighting* after regular work hours
    C. *rotate* overtime as much as possible among employees willing to work additional
hours
    D. *assign* overtime to those employees who take frequent long weekend vacations

2. The consistent delegation of authority by you to experienced and reliable subordinates in   2.____
your work group is generally considered

    A. *undesirable*, because your authority in the group may be threatened by an unscru-
pulous subordinate
    B. *undesirable*, because it demonstrates that you cannot handle your own workload
    C. *desirable*, because it shows that you believe that you have been accepted by your
subordinates
    D. *desirable*, because the development of subordinates creates opportunities for
assuming broader responsibilities yourself

3. The MOST effective way for you to deal with a false rumor circulating among your subor-   3.____
dinates is to

    A. have a trusted subordinate state a counter-rumor
    B. recommend disciplinary action against the *rumor mongers*
    C. point out to your subordinates that rumors degrade both listener and initiator
    D. furnish your subordinates with sufficient authentic information

4. Two of your subordinates tell you about a mistake they made in a report that has already   4.____
been sent the top management.
Which of the following questions is *most likely* to elicit the MOST valuable information
from your subordinates?

    A. Who is responsible?
    B. How can we explain this to top management?
    C. How did it happen?
    D. Why weren't you more careful?

5. Assume that you are responsible for implementing major changes in work flow patterns   5.____
and personnel assignments in the unit of which you are in charge.
The *one* of the following actions which is *most likely* to secure the willing cooperation
of those persons who will have to change their assignmentsis

A. having the top administrators of the agency urge their cooperation at a group meeting
B. issuing very detailed and carefully planned instructions to the affected employees regarding the changes
C. integrating employee participation into the planning of the changes
D. reminding the affected employees that career advancement depends upon compliance with organizational objectives

6. Of the following, the BEST reason for using face-to-face communication *instead of* written communication is that face-to-face communication   6._____

    A. allows for immediate feedback
    B. is more credible
    C. enables greater use of detail and illustration
    D. is more polite

7. Of the following, the *most likely* DISADVANTAGE of giving detailed instructions when assigning a task to a subordinate is that such instructions may   7._____

    A. conflict with the subordinate's ideas of how the task should be done
    B. reduce standardization of work performance
    C. cause confusion in the mind of the subordinate
    D. inhibit the development of new procedures by the subordinate

8. Assume that you are a supervisor of a unit consisting of a number of subordinates and   8._____
that one subordinate, whose work is otherwise acceptable, keeps on making errors in one particular task assigned to him in rotation. This task consists of routine duties which all your subordinates should be able to perform.
Of the following, the BEST way for you to handle this situation is to

    A. do the task yourself when the erring employee is scheduled to perform it and assign this employee other duties
    B. reorganize work assignments so that the task in question is no longer performed in rotation but assigned full-time to your most capable subordinate
    C. find out why this subordinate keeps on making the errors in question and see that he learns how to do the task properly
    D. maintain a well-documented record of such errors and, when the evidence is overwhelming, recommend appropriate disciplinary action

9. In the past, Mr. T, one of your subordinates, had been generally withdrawn and suspicious of others, but he had produced acceptable work. However, Mr. T has lately started   9._____
to get into arguments with his fellow workers during which he displays intense rage. Friction between this subordinate and the others in your unit is mounting and the unit's work is suffering.
Of the following, which would be the BEST way for you to handle this situation?

    A. Rearrange work schedules and assignments so as to give Mr. T no cause for complaint
    B. Instruct the other workers to avoid Mr. T and not to respond to any abuse
    C. Hold a unit meeting and appeal for harmony and submergence of individual differences in the interest of work
    D. Maintain a record of incidents and explore with Mr. T the possibility of seeking professional help

10. You are responsible for seeing to it that your unit is functioning properly in the accomplishment of its budgeted goals.
Which of the following will provide the LEAST information on how well you are accomplishing such goals?

    A. Measurement of employee performance
    B. Identification of alternative goals
    C. Detection of employee errors
    D. Preparation of unit reports

10.____

11. Some employees see an agency training program as a threat. Of the following, the *most likely* reason for such an employee attitude toward training is that the employee involved feel that

    A. some trainers are incompetent
    B. training rarely solves real work-a-day problems
    C. training may attempt to change comfortable behavior patterns
    D. training sessions are boring

11.____

12. Of the following, the CHIEF characteristic which distinguishes a *good* supervisor from a *poor* supervisor is the *good* supervisor's

    A. ability to favorably impress others
    B. unwillingness to accept monotony or routine
    C. ability to deal constructively with problem situations
    D. strong drive to overcome opposition

12.____

13. Of the following, the MAIN disadvantage of on-the-job training is that, *generally,*

    A. special equipment may be needed
    B. production may be slowed down
    C. the instructor must maintain an individual relationship with the trainee
    D. the on-the-job instructor must be better qualified than the classroom instructor

13.____

14. All of the following are *correct* methods for a supervisor to use in connection with employee discipline EXCEPT

    A. trying not to be too lenient or too harsh
    B. informing employees of the rules and the penalties for violations of the rules
    C. imposing discipline immediately after the violation is discovered
    D. making sure, when you apply discipline, that the employee understands that you do not want to do it

14.____

15. Of the following, the MAIN reason for a supervisor to establish standard procedures for his unit is to

    A. increase the motivation for his subordinates
    B. make it easier for the subordinates to submit to authority
    C. reduce the number of times that his subordinates have to consult him
    D. reduce the number of mistakes that his subordinates will make

15.____

16. Of the following, the BEST reason for using form letters in correspondence is that they are   16.____

    A. concise and businesslike
    B. impersonal in tone
    C. uniform in appearance
    D. economical for large mailings

17. The use of loose-leaf office manuals for the guidance of employees on office policy, orga-   17.____
    nization, and office procedures has won wide acceptance.
    The MAIN advantage of the loose-leaf format is that it

    A. allows speedy reference
    B. facilitates revisions and changes
    C. includes a complete index
    D. presents a professional appearance

18. Office forms sometimes consist of several copies, each of a different color.   18.____
    The MAIN reason for using *different* colors is to

    A. make a favorable impression on the users of the form
    B. distinguish each copy from the others
    C. facilitate the preparation of legible carbon copies
    D. reduce cost, since using colored stock permits recycling of paper

19. Which of the following is the BEST justification for obtaining a photocopying machine for   19.____
    the office?

    A. A photocopying machine can produce an unlimited number of copies at a low fixed
       cost per copy.
    B. Employees need little training in operating a photocopying machine.
    C. Office costs will be reduced and efficiency increased.
    D. The legibility of a photocopy generally is superior to copy produced by any other
       office duplicating device.

20. Which one of the following should be the most IMPORTANT overall consideration when   20.____
    preparing a recommendation to automate a large-scale office activity?
    The

    A. number of models of automated equipment available
    B. benefits and costs of automation
    C. fears and resistance of affected employees
    D. experience of offices which have automated similar activities

21. A tickler file is MOST appropriate for filing materials   21.____

    A. chronologically according to date they were received
    B. alphabetically by name
    C. alphabetically by subject
    D. chronologically according to date they should be followed up

54

22. Which of the following is the BEST reason for decentralizing rather than centralizing the use of duplicating machines?   22.____

    A. Developing and retaining efficient deplicating machine operators
    B. Facilitating supervision of duplicating services
    C. Motivating employees to produce legible duplicated copies
    D. Placing the duplicating machines where they are most convenient and most frequently used

23. Window envelopes are sometimes considered preferable to individually addressed envelopes PRIMARILY because   23.____

    A. window envelopes are available in standard sizes for all purposes
    B. window envelopes are more attractive and official-looking
    C. the use of window envelopes eliminates the risk of inserting a letter in the wrong envelope
    D. the use of window envelopes requires neater typing

24. In planning the layout of a new office, the utilization of space and the arrangement of staff, furnishings and equipment should *usually* be MOST influenced by the   24.____

    A. gross square footage
    B. status differences in the chain of command
    C. framework of informal relationships among employees
    D. activities to be performed

25. When delegating responsibility for an assignment to a subordinate, it is MOST important that you   25.____

    A. retain all authority necessary to complete the assignment
    B. make your self generally available for consultation with the subordinate
    C. inform your superiors that you are no longer responsible for the assignment
    D. decrease the number of subordinates whom you have to supervise

---

KEY (CORRECT ANSWERS)

1.	C	11.	C	21.	D
2.	D	12.	C	22.	D
3.	D	13.	B	23.	C
4.	D	14.	D	24.	D
5.	C	15.	C	25.	B
6.	A	16.	D		
7.	D	17.	B		
8.	C	18.	B		
9.	D	19.	C		
10.	B	20.	B		

TEST 2

DIRECTIONS: Each question or incomplete statement is followed by several suggested answers or completions. Select the one that BEST answers the question or completes the statement. *PRINT THE LETTER OF THE CORRECT ANSWER IN THE SPACE AT THE RIGHT.*

Questions 1-5.

DIRECTIONS: Answer Questions 1 through 5 on the basis of the following passage.

The most effective control mechanism to prevent gross incompetence on the part of public employees is a good personnel program. The personnel officer in the line departments and the central personnel agency should exert positive leadership to raise levels of performance. Although the key factor is the quality of the personnel recruited, staff members other than personnel officers can make important contributions to efficiency. Administrative analysts, now employed in many agencies, make detailed studies of organization and procedures, with the purpose of eliminating delays, waste, and other inefficiencies. Efficiency is, however, more than a question of good organization and procedures; it is also the product of the attitudes and values of the public employees. Personal motivation can provide the will to be efficient. The best management studies will not result in substantial improvement of the performance of those employees who feel no great urge to work up to their abilities.

1. The passage indicates that the *key* factor in preventing gross incompetence of public employees is the   1.____

    A. hiring of administrative analysts to assist personnel people
    B. utilization of effective management studies
    C. overlapping of responsibility
    D. quality of the employees hired

2. According to the above passage, the central personnel agency staff *should*   2.____

    A. work more closely with administrative analysts in the line departments than with personnel afficers
    B. make a serious effort to avoid jurisdictional conflicts with personnel officers in line departments
    C. contribute to improving the quality of work of public employees
    D. engage in a comprehensive program to change the public's negative image of public employees

3. The passage indicates that efficiency in an organization can BEST be brought about by   3.____

    A. eliminating ineffective control mechanisms
    B. instituting sound organizational procedures
    C. promoting competent personnel
    D. recruiting people with desire to do good work

4. According to the passage, the *purpose* of administrative analysis in a public agency is to   4.____

    A. prevent injustice to the public employee
    B. promote the efficiency of the agency
    C. protect the interests of the public
    D. ensure the observance of procedural due process

5. The passage implies that a considerable rise in the quality of work of public employees can be brought about by   5.____

   A. encouraging positive employee attitudes toward work
   B. controlling personnel officers who exceed their powers
   C. creating warm personal associations among public employees in an agency
   D. closing loopholes in personnel organization and procedures

6. Typist X can type 20 forms per hour and Typist I can type 30 forms per hour. If there are 30 forms to be typed and both typists are put to work on the job, *how soon* should they be expected to finish the work? _____ minutes.   6.____

   A. 32   B. 34   C. 36   D. 38

7. Assume that there were 18 working days in February and that the six clerks in your unit had the following number of absences: 7.____

                Clerk F - 3 absences
                Clerk G - 2 absences
                Clerk H - 8 absences
                Clerk I - 1 absence
                Clerk J - 0 absences
                Clerk K - 5 absences

The average percentage attendance for the six clerks in your unit in February was, *most nearly,*

   A. 80%   B. 82%   C. 84%   D. 86%

8. A certain employee is paid at the rate of $7.50 per hour, with time-and-a-half for overtime. Hours in excess of 40 hours a week count as overtime. During the past week the employee put in 48 working hours. The employee's gross wages for the week are, *most nearly,*   8.____

   A. $330   B. $350   C. $370   D. $390

9. You are making a report on the number of inside and outside calls handled by a particular switchboard. Over a 15-day period, the total number of all inside and outside calls handled by the switchboard was 5,760. The average number of inside calls per day was 234. You cannot find one day's tally of outside calls, but the total number of outside calls for the other fourteen days was 2,065. From this information, how many *outside calls* must have been reported on the missing tally?   9.____

   A. 175   B. 185   C. 195   D. 205

10. A floor plan has been prepared for a new building, drawn to a scale of 3/4 inch = 1 foot. A certain area is drawn 1 and 1/2 feet long and 6 inches wide on the floor plan. What are the *actual* dimensions of this area in the new building? _____ feet long and _____ feet wide.   10.____

   A. 21; 8   B. 24; 8   C. 27; 9   D. 30; 9

Questions 11 - 15.

DIRECTIONS: In answering Questions 11 through 15, assume that you are in charge of public information for an office which issues reports and answers questions from
other offices and from the public on changes in land use. The charts below
represent comparative land use in four neighborhoods. The area of each
neighborhood is expressed in city blocks. Assume that all city blocks are the
same size.

NEIGHBORHOOD A - 16 CITY BLOCKS   NEIGHBORHOOD B - 24 CITY BLOCKS

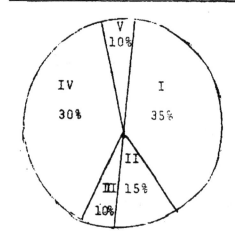 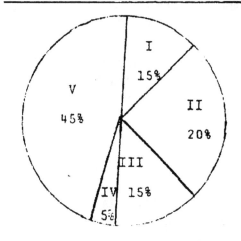

NEIGHBORHOOD C - 20 CITY BLOCKS   NEIGHBORHOOD D - 12 CITY BLOCKS

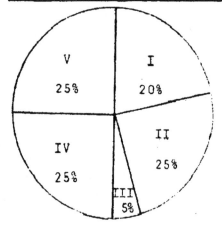 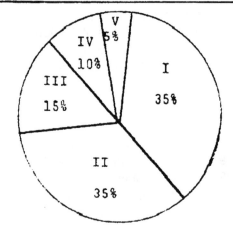

KEY: I- one- and two-family houses   III. Office buildings
       II- Apartment buildings   IV. Rental stores
                          V. Factories and warehouses

11. In how many of these neighborhoods does residential use (categories I and II together)   11.____
     account for at least 50% of the land use?

     A. One   B. Two   C. Three   D. Four

12. Which neighborhood has the largest land area occupied by apartment buildings? Neigh-   12.____
     borhood _____ .

     A. A   B. B   C. C   D. D

13. In which neighborhood is the largest percentage of the land devoted to both office buildings and retail stores? Neighborhood _____ .   13.____

    A. A   B. B   C. C   D. D

14. What is the difference, to the nearest city block, between the amount of land devoted to retail stores in Neighborhood B and the amount devoted to similar use in Neighborhood C? _____ block(s).   14.____

    A. 1   B. 2   C. 4   D. 6

15. Which one of the following types of buildings occupies the same amount of land area in Neighborhood B as the amount of land area occupied by retail stores in Neighborhood A?   15.____

    A. Factories and warehouses
    B. Office buildings
    C. Retail stores
    D. Apartment buildings

Questions 16 - 20.

DIRECTIONS: Answer Questions 16 through 20 on the basis of the following passage.

For a period of nearly fifteen years, beginning in the mid-1950's, higher education sustained a phenomenal rate of growth. The factors principally responsible were continuing improvement in the rate of college entrance by high school graduates, a 50-percent increase in the size of the college-age (eighteen to twenty-one) group, and - until about 1967 - a rapid expansion of university research activity supported by the federal government.

Today, as one looks ahead fifteen years to the year 2020, it is apparent that each of these favorable stimuli will either be abated or turn into a negative factor. The rate of growth of the college-age group has already diminished, and from 2010 to 2015 the size of the college-age group will shrink annually almost as fast as it grew from 1965 to 1970. From 2015 to 2020, this annual decrease will slow down so that by 2020 the age-group will be about the same size as it was in 2019. This substantial net decrease in the size of the college-age group over the next fifteen years will dramatically affect college enrollments since, currently, 83 percent of undergraduates are twenty-one and under, and another 11 percent are twenty-one to twenty-four.

16. Which one of the following factors is NOT mentioned in the above passage as contributing to the high rate of growth of higner education?   16.____

    A. A larger increase in the size of the eighteen to twenty-one age group
    B. The equalization of educational opportunities among socio-economic groups
    C. The federal budget impact on research and development spending in the higher education sector
    D. The increasing rate at which high school graduates enter college

17. Based on the information in the above passage, the size of the college-age group in 2020 will be 17.____

    A. larger than it was in 2019
    B. larger than it was in 2005
    C. smaller than it was in 2015
    D. about the same as it was in 2010

18. According to the above passage, the tremendous rate of growth of higher education started around 18.____

    A. 1950   B. 1955   C. 1960   D. 1965

19. The percentage of undergraduates who are over age 24 is, *most nearly,* 19.____

    A. 6%   B. 8%   C. 11%   D. 17%

20. Which one of the following conclusions can be substantiated by the information given in the above passage? 20.____

    A. The college-age group will be about the same size in 2010 as it was in 1965.
    B. The annual decrease in the size of the college-age group from 2010 to 2015 will be about the same as the annual increase from 1965 to 1970.
    C. The overall decrease in the size of the college-age group from 2010 to 2015 will be followed by an overall increase in its size from 2015 to 2020.
    D. The size of the college-age group will decrease at a fairly constant rate from 1995 to 2010.

21. Because higher status is important to many employees, they will often make an effort to achieve it as an end in itself. 21.____
Of the following, the BEST course of action for the supervisor to take on the basis of the preceding statement is to

    A. attach higher status to that behavior of subordinates which is directed toward reaching the goals of the organization
    B. avoid showing sympathy toward subordinates' wishes for increased wages, improved working conditions, or other benefits
    C. foster interpersonal competitiveness among subordinates so that personal friendliness is replaced by the desire to protect individual status
    D. reprimand subordinates whenever their work is in some way unsatisfactory in order to adjust their status accordingly

22. Assume that a large office in a certain organization operates long hours and is thus on two shifts with a slight overlap. Those employees, including supervisors, who are most productive are given their choice of shifts. The earlier shift is considered preferable by most employees . 22.____
As a result of this method of assignment, which of the following is *most likely* to result?

    A. Most non-supervisory employees will be assigned to the late shift; most supervisors will be assigned to the early shift.
    B. Most supervisors will be assigned to the late shift; most non-supervisory employees will be assigned to the early shift.
    C. The early shift will be more productive than the late shift.
    D. The late shift will be more productive than the early shift.

23. Assume that a supervisor of a unit in which the employees are of avera.ge friendliness
tells a newly-hired employee on her first day that her co-workers are very friendly. The
other employees hear his remarks to the new employee.
Which of the following is the most *likely* result of this action of the supervisor? The

23.____

    A. newly-hired employee will tend to feel less friendly than if the supervisor had said
nothing
    B. newly-hired employee will tend to believe that her co-workers are very friendly
    C. other employees will tend to feel less friendly toward one another
    D. other employees will tend to see the newly-hired employee as insincerely friendly

24. A recent study of employee absenteeism showed that, although unscheduled absence
for part of a week is relatively high for young employees, unscheduled absence for a full
week is low. However, although full-week unscheduled absence is least frequent for the
youngest employees, the frequency of such absence increases as the age of employees
increases.
Which of the following statements is the MOST logical explanation for the greater full-
week absenteeism among older employees?

24.____

    A. *Older* employees are more likely to be males.
    B. *Older* employees are more likely to have more relatively serious illnesses.
    C. *Younger* employees are more likely to take longer vacations.
    D. *Younger* employees are more likely to be newly-hired.

25. An employee can be motivated to fulfill his needs as he sees them. He is not motivated
by what others think he ought to have, but what he himself wants. Which of the following
statements follows MOST logically from the foregoing viewpoint?

25.____

    A. A person's different traits may be separately classified, but they are all part of one
system comprising a whole person.
    B. Every job, however simple, entitles the person who does it to proper respect and
recognition of his unique aspirations and abilities.
    C. No matter what equipment and facilities an organization has, they cannot be put to
use except by people who have been motivated.
    D. To an observer, a person's need may be unrealistic but they are still controlling.

KEY (CORRECT ANSWERS)

1.	D		11.	B
2.	C		12.	C
3.	D		13.	A
4.	B		14.	C
5.	A		15.	D
6.	C		16.	B
7.	B		17.	C
8.	D		18.	B
9.	B		19.	A
10.	B		20.	B

21.	A
22.	C
23.	B
24.	B
25.	D

———

EXAMINATION SECTION
TEST 1

DIRECTIONS: Each question or incomplete statement is followed by several suggested
answers or completions. Select the one that BEST answers the question or
completes the statement. *PRINT THE LETTER OF THE CORRECT ANSWER
IN THE SPACE AT THE RIGHT.*

1. Assume that you are a supervisor of a unit which is about to start work on an urgent job.   1._____
One of your subordinates starts to talk to you about the urgent job but seems not to be
saying what is really on his mind.
What is the BEST thing for you to say under these circumstances?

    A.   *I'm not sure I understand. Can you explain that?*
    B.   *Please come to the point. We haven't got all day.*
    C.   *What is it? Can't you see I'm busy?*
    D.   *Haven't you got work to do? What do you want?*

2. Assume that you have recently been assigned a new subordinate. You have explained to   2._____
this subordinate how to fill out certain forms which will constitute the major portion of her
job. After the first day, you find that she has filled out the forms correctly but has not completed as many as most other workers normally complete in a day.
Of the following, the MOST appropriate action for you to take is to

    A.   tell the subordinate how many forms she is expected to complete
    B.   instruct the subordinate in the correct method of filling out the forms
    C.   monitor the subordinate's production to see if she improves
    D.   reassign the job of filling out the forms to a more experienced worker in the unit

3. One of the problems commonly met by the supervisor is the *touchy* employee who imag-   3._____
ines slights when none are intended.
Of the following, the BEST way to deal with such an employee is to

    A.   ignore him, until he sees the error of his behavior
    B.   frequently reassure him of his value as a person
    C.   advise him that oversensitive people rarely get promoted
    D.   issue written instructions to him to avoid misinterpretation

4. The understanding supervisor should recognize that a certain amount of anxiety is com-   4._____
mon to all newly-hired employees. If you are a supervisor of a unit and a newly-hired
employee has been assigned to you, you can usually assume that the LEAST likely
worry that the new employee has is worry about

    A.   the job and the standards required in the job
    B.   his acceptance by the other people in your unit
    C.   the difficulty of advancing to top positions in the agency
    D.   your fairness in evaluating his work

5. In assigning work to subordinates, it is often desirable for you to tell them the overall or ultimate objective of the assignment.
   Of the following, the BEST reason for telling them the objective is that it will

   5._____

   A. assure them that you know what you are doing
   B. eliminate most of the possible complaints about the assignment
   C. give them confidence in their ability to do the assignment
   D. help them to make decisions consistent with the objective

6. Generally a supervisor wishes to increase the likelihood that instructions given to subordinates will be carried out properly.
   Of the following, the MOST important action for the supervisor to take to accomplish this objective when giving instructions to subordinates is to

   6._____

   A. tailor the instructions to fit the interests of the subordinate
   B. use proper timing in giving the instruction
   C. make sure that the subordinates understand the instructions
   D. include only those instructions that are essential to the task at hand

7. Suppose that a supervisor, because of his heavy workload, has decided to delegate to his subordinates some of the duties that he has been performing.
   Of the following attitudes of the supervisor, the one that is LEAST conducive toward effective delegation is his belief that

   7._____

   A. his subordinates will make some mistakes in performing these duties
   B. controls will be necessary to make sure the work is done
   C. performance of these duties may be slowed down temporarily
   D. much of his time will be spent supervising performance of these duties

8. In attempting to determine why one of his subordinates has frequently been coming to work late, a supervisor begins an interview with the subordinate by asking her whether everything is all right on the job and at home. The BEST of the following reasons for beginning the interview in this manner is that a question specifically about the reason for the lateness

   8._____

   A. might indicate insecurity on the part of the supervisor
   B. might limit the responses of the subordinate
   C. will offend the subordinate
   D. might reveal the purpose of the interview

9. Of the following, the BEST use to which a supervisor should put his knowledge of human relations is to

   9._____

   A. enhance his image among his subordinates
   B. improve interpersonal relationships with the organization
   C. prompt the organization to an awareness of mental health
   D. resolve technical differences of opinion among employees

10. Which of the following types of information would come tribute LEAST to a measure of the quality of working conditions for employees in various jobs?

    10.____

    A. Data reflecting a view of working conditions as seen through the eyes of workers
    B. Objective data relating to problems in working conditions, such as occupational safety statistics
    C. The considered opinion of recognized specialists in relevant fields
    D. The impressionistic accounts of journalists in feature articles

Questions 11–15

DIRECTIONS: Questions 11 through 15 each consist of a sentence which may or may not be an example of good English usage. Consider grammar, punctuation, spelling, capitalization, verbosity, awkwardness, etc. Examine each sentence, and then choose the correct statement about it from the four choices below it. If the English usage in the sentence is better as given than with any of the changes suggested in options B, C, or D, choose option A. Do NOT choose an option that will change the meaning of the sentence.

11. The clerk could have completed the assignment on time if he knows where these materials were located.

    11.____

    A. This is an example of acceptable writing.
    B. The word *knows* should be replaced by *had known*.
    C. The word *were* should be replaced by *had been*.
    D. The words *where these materials were located* should be replaced by *the location of these materials*.

12. All employees should be given safety training. Not just those who have accidents.

    12.____

    A. This is an example of acceptable writing.
    B. The period after the word *training* should be changed to a colon.
    C. The period after the word *training* should be changed to a semicolon, and the first letter of the word *Not* should be changed to a small *n*.
    D. The period after the word *training* should be changed to a comma, and the first letter of the word *Not* should be changed to a small *n*.

13. This proposal is designed to promote employee awareness of the suggestion program, to encourage employee participation in the program, and to increase the number of suggestions submitted.

    13.____

    A. This is an example of acceptable writing.
    B. The word *proposal* should be spelled *preposal*.
    C. the words *to increase the number of suggestions submitted* should be changed to *an increase in the number of suggestions is expected*.
    D. The word *promote* should be changed to *enhance* and the word *increase* should be changed to *add to*.

14. The introduction of inovative managerial techniques should be preceded by careful anal-   14.____
    ysis of the specific circumstances and conditions in each department.

    A. This is an example of acceptable writing.
    B. The word *techniques* should be spelled *techneques*.
    C. The word *inovative* should be spelled *innovative*.
    D. A comma should be placed after the word *circumstance* and after the word *condi-tions*.

15. This occurrence indicates that such criticism embarrasses him.   15.____

    A. This is an example of acceptable writing.
    B. The word *occurrence* should be spelled *occurence*.
    C. The word *criticism* should be spelled *criticizm*.
    D. The word *embarrasses* should be spelled *embarasses*.

Questions 16–18.

DIRECTIONS: Questions 16 through 18 each consist of four sentences. Choose the one sentence in each set of four that would be BEST for a *formal* letter or report. Consider grammar and appropriate usage.

16.   A. Most all the work he completed before he become ill.   16.____
    B. He completed most of the work before becoming ill.
    C. Prior to him becoming ill his work was mostly completed.
    D. Before he became ill most of the work he had completed.

17.   A. Being that the report lacked a clearly worded recomendation, it did not matter that   17.____
       it contained enough information.
    B. There was enough information in the report, although it, including the recom-
       mendation, were not clearly worded.
    C. Although the report contained enough information, it did not have a clearly
       worded recommendation.
    D. Though the report did not have a recommendation that was clearly worded, and
       the information therein contained was enough.

18.   A. Having already overlooked the important mistakes, the ones which she found were   18.____
       not as important toward the end of the letter.
    B. Toward the end of the letter she had already overlooked the important mistakes,
       so that which she had found were not as important.
    C. The mistakes which she had already overlooked were not as important as those
       which near the end of letter she had found.
    D. The mistakes which she found near the end of the letter were not as important
       as those which she had already overlooked.

19. Examine the following sentence, and then choose from below the words which should be   19.____
    inserted in the blank spaces to produce the best sentence.
    The unit has exceeded _____ goals and the employees are satisfied
    with _____ accomplishments.

    A. their, it's   B. it's, it's
    C. its, there   D. its, their

20. Examine the following sentence, and then choose from below the words which should be   20.____
    inserted in the blank spaces to produce the best sentence.
        Research indicates that employees who _____ no opportunity for close social rela-
    tionships often find their work unsatisfying, and this _____ of satisfaction often
    reflects itself in low production.

    A. have, lack   B. have, excess
    C. has, lack   D. has, excess

KEY (CORRECT ANSWERS)

1.	A	11.	B
2.	C	12.	D
3.	B	13.	A
4.	C	14.	C
5.	D	15.	A
6.	C	16.	B
7.	D	17.	C
8.	B	18.	D
9.	B	19.	D
10.	D	20.	A

TEST 2

DIRECTIONS: Each question or incomplete statement is followed by several suggested answers or completions. Select the one that BEST answers the question or completes the statement. *PRINT THE LETTER OF THE CORRECT ANSWER IN THE SPACE AT THE RIGHT.*

1. Of the following, the GREATEST *pitfall* in interviewing is that the result may be effected by the

    A. bias of the interviewee
    B. bias of the interviewer
    C. educational level of the interviewee
    D. educational level of the interviewer

    1.____

2. Assume that you have been asked to interview each of several students who have been hired to work part-time. Which of the following could *ordinarily* be accomplished LEAST effectively in such an interview?

    A. Providing information about the organization or institution in which the students will be working
    B. Directing the students to report for work each afternoon at specified times
    C. Determining experience and background of the students so that appropriate assignments can be made
    D. Changing the attitudes of the students toward the importance of parental controls

    2.____

3. Assume that someone you are interviewing is reluctant to give you certain information. He would *probably* be MORE responsive if you show him that

    A. all the other persons you interviewed provided you with the information
    B. it would serve his own best interests to give you the information
    C. the information is very important to you
    D. you are businesslike and take a no-nonsense approach

    3.____

4. Taking notes while you are interviewing someone is *most likely* to

    A. arouse doubts as to your trustworthiness
    B. give the interviewee confidence in your ability
    C. insure that you record the facts you think are important
    D. make the responses of the interviewee unreliable

    4.____

5. Assume that you have been asked to get all the pertinent information from an employee who claims that she witnessed a robbery.
   Which of the following questions is LEAST likely to influence the witness's response?

    A. *Can you describe the robber's hair?*
    B. *Did the robber have a lot of hair?*
    C. *Was the robber's hair black or brown?*
    D. *Was the robber's hair very dark?*

6. If you are to interview several applicants for jobs and rate them on five different factors on a scale of 1 to 5, you should be MOST careful to *insure* that your   6.____

    A. rating on one factor does not influence your rating on another factor
    B. ratings on all factors are interrelated with a minimum of variation
    C. overall evaluation for employment exactly reflects the arithmetic average of your ratings
    D. overall evaluation for employment is unrelated to your individual ratings

7. In answering questions asked by students, faculty, and the public, it is MOST important that   7.____

    A. you indicate your source of information
    B. you are not held responsible for the answers
    C. the facts you give be accurate
    D. the answers cover every possible aspect of each question

8. One of the applicants for a menial job is a tall, stooped, husky individual with a low forehead, narrow eyes, a protruding chin, and a tendency to keep his mouth open.
In interviewing him, you *should*   8.____

    A. check him more carefully than the other applicants regarding criminal background
    B. disregard any skills he might have for other jobs which are vacant
    C. make your vocabulary somewhat simpler than with the other applicants
    D. make no assumption regarding his ability on the basis of his appearance

9. Of the following, the BEST approach for you to use at the beginning of an interview with a job applicant is to   9.____

    A. caution him to use his time economically and to get to the point
    B. ask him how long he intends to remain on the job if hired
    C. make some pleasant remarks to put him at ease
    D. emphasize the importance of the interview in obtaining the job

10. Of the following, the BEST reason for conducting an *exit interview* with an employee is to   10.____

    A. make certain that he returns all identification cards and office keys
    B. find out why he is leaving
    C. provide a useful training device for the exit interviewer
    D. discover if his initial hiring was in error

11. Suppose that a visitor to an office asks a receptionist for a specific person by name. The person is available, but the visitor refuses to state the purpose of the visit, saying that it is *personal.*
Which of the following is the MOST appropriate response for the receptionist to make?   11.____

    A. *Does M_____ know you?*
    B. *I'm sorry, M_____ is busy.*
    C. *M _____ won't be able to help you unless you're more specific.*
    D. *M_____ is not able to see you.*

12. When writing a reply to a letter you received, it is proper to mention the subject of the let- 12.____
ter.
However, you should ordinarily NOT summarize the contents or repeat statements
made in the letter you received PRIMARILY because

    A. a letter writer answers people, not letters
    B. direct answers will help you avoid sounding pompous
    C. the response will thus be more confidential
    D. the sender usually knows what he or she wrote

13. Assume that you are a supervisor in an office which gets approximately equal quantities 13.____
of urgent work and work that is not urgent. The volume of work is high during some periods and low during others.
In order to level out the fluctuations in workload, it would be BEST for you to schedule
work so that

    A. urgent work which comes up in a period of high work volume can be handled expe-
ditiously by the use of voluntary overtime
    B. urgent work is postponed for completion in periods of low volume
    C. work is completed as it comes into the office, except that when urgent work arises,
other work is laid aside temporarily
    D. work is completed chronologically, that is, on the basis of *first in, first out*

14. Suppose that a supervisor sets up a pick-up and delivery messenger system to cover 14.____
several nearby buildings. Each building has at least one station for both pick-up and
delivery. Three messenger trips are scheduled for each day, and the messenger is
instructed to make pick-ups and deliveries at the same time.
In this situation, telling the messenger to visit each pick-up and delivery station even
though there is nothing to deliver to it is

    A. *advisable,* messengers are generally not capable of making decisions for them-
selves
    B. *advisable,* there may be material for the messenger to pick up
    C. *inadvisable,* the system must be made flexible to meet variable workload condi-
tions
    D. *inadvisable,* postponing the visit until there is something to deliver is more efficient

15. You, as a unit head, have been asked to submit budget estimates of staff, equipment and 15.____
supplies in terms of programs for your unit for the coming fiscal year. In addition to their
use in planning, such unit budget estimates can be BEST used to

    A. reveal excessive costs in operations
    B. justify increases in the debt limit
    C. analyze employee salary adjustments
    D. predict the success of future programs

Questions 16–21.

DIRECTIONS: Questions 16 through 21 involve calculations of annual grade averages for college students who have just completed their junior year. These averages are to be based on the following table showing the number of credit hours for each student during the year at each of the grade levels: A, B, C, D, and F. How these letter grades may be translated into numerical grades is indicated in the first column of the table.

Grade Value	Credit Hours –Junior Year					
	King	Lewis	Martin	Nonkin	Ottly	Perry
A=95	12	12	9	15	6	3
B=85	9	12	9	12	18	6
C=75	6	6	9	3	3	21
D=65	3	3	3	3	–	–
F=0	–	–	3	–	–	–

Calculating a grade average for an individual student is a 4-step process:
   I.   Multiply each grade value by the number of credit hours for which the student received that grade.
   II.   Add these multiplication products for each student.
   III.   Add the student's total credit hours.
   IV.   Divide the multiplication product total by the total number of credit hours.
   V.   Round the result, if there is a decimal place, to the nearest whole number. A number ending in .5 would be rounded to the next higher number.

EXAMPLE

Using student King's grades as an example, his grade average can be calculated by going through the following four steps:

I.   95   x   12   =   1140   III.   12
     85   x   9   =   765   9
     75   x   6   =   450   6
     65   x   3   =   195   3
      0   x   0   =   0   0
                                          30   total credit hours

II.   Total   =   2550   IV.   Divide 2550 by 30: $\frac{2550}{30} = 85$.

King's grade average is 85.
   Answer Questions 16 through 21 on the basis of the information given above.

16.   The grade average of Lewis is   16._____

      A.   83   B.   84   C.   85   D.   86

17.   The grade average of Martin is   17._____

      A.   72   B.   73   C.   74   D.   75

18.   The grade average of Nonkin is   18._____

      A.   85   B.   86   C.   87   D.   88

19. Student Ottly must attain a grade average of 90 in each of his years in college to be accepted into the graduate school of his choice.
If, in summer school during his junior year, he takes two 3–credit courses and receives a grade of 95 in each one, his grade average for his junior year will then be, *most nearly,*

    A. 87   B. 88   C. 89   D. 90

19._____

20. If Perry takes an additional 3–credit course during the year and receives a grade of 95, his grade average will be increased to approximately

    A. 79   B. 80   C. 81   D. 82

20._____

21. What has been the *effect* of automation in data processing on the planning of managerial objectives?

    A. Paperwork can be virtually eliminated from the planning process.
    B. The information on which such planning is based can be more precise and up-to-date.
    C. Planning must be done much more frequently because of the constantly changing nature of the objectives.
    D. Planning can be done much less frequently because of the increased stability of objectives.

21._____

22. Which of the following is the BEST reason for budgeting a new calculating machine for an office?

    A. The clerks in the office often make mistakes in adding.
    B. The machine would save time and money.
    C. It was budgeted last year but never received.
    D. All the other offices have calculating machines.

22._____

23. Which of the following is *most likely* to reduce the volume of paperwork in a unit responsible for preparing a large number of reports?

    A. Changing the office layout so that there will be a minimum of backtracking and delay.
    B. Acquiring additional adding and calculating machines.
    C. Consolidating some of the reports.
    D. Inaugurating a *records retention* policy to reduce the length of time office papers are retained.

23._____

24. With regard to typed correspondence received by most offices, which of the following is the GREATEST problem?

    A. Verbosity   B. Illegibility
    C. Improper folding   D. Excessive copies

24._____

25. Of the following, the GREATEST advantage of electronic typewriters over electric type-writers is that they *usually*

    A. are less expensive to repair
    B. are smaller and lighter
    C. produce better looking copy
    D. require less training for the typist

25.____

KEY (CORRECT ANSWERS)

1.	B		11.	A
2.	D		12.	D
3.	B		13.	C
4.	C		14.	B
5.	A		15.	A
6.	A		16.	C
7.	C		17.	D
8.	D		18.	C
9.	C		19.	B
10.	B		20.	B

21.	B
22.	B
23.	C
24.	A
25.	C

EXAMINATION SECTION
TEST 1

DIRECTIONS: Each question or incomplete statement is followed by several suggested answers or completions. Select the one that BEST answers the question or completes the statement. *PRINT THE LETTER OF THE CORRECT ANSWER IN THE SPACE AT THE RIGHT.*

1. A push-button telephone with six buttons, one of which is a *hold* button, is often used when more than one outside line is needed.
If you are talking on one line of this type of telephone when another call comes in, what is the procedure to follow if you want to answer the second call but keep the first call on the line? Push the

    A. *hold* button at the same time as you push the *pickup* button of the ringing line
    B. *hold* button and then push the *pickup* button of the ringing line
    C. *pickup* button of the ringing line and then push the *hold* button
    D. *pickup* button of the ringing line and push the *hold* button when you return to the original line

1.____

2. Suppose that you are asked to prepare a petty cash statement for March. The original and one copy are to go to the personnel office. One copy is to go to the fiscal office, and another copy is to go to your supervisor. The last copy is for your files.
In preparing the statement and the copies, how many sheets of copy paper should you use?

    A. 3   B. 4   C. 5   D. 8

2.____

3. Which one of the following is the LEAST important advantage of putting the subject of a letter in the heading to the right of the address?
It

    A. makes filing of the copy easier
    B. makes more space available in the body of the letter
    C. simplifies distribution of letters
    D. simplifies determination of the subject of the letter

3.____

4. Of the following, the MOST efficient way to put 100 copies of a one-page letter into 9 1/2" x 4 1/8" envelopes for mailing is to fold _____ into an envelope.

    A. each letter and insert it immediately after folding
    B. each letter separately until all 100 are folded; then insert each one
    C. the 100 letters two at a time, then separate them and insert each one
    D. two letters together, slip them apart, and insert each one

4.____

5. When preparing papers for filing, it is NOT desirable to

    A. smooth papers that are wrinkled
    B. use paper clips to keep related papers together in the files
    C. arrange the papers in the order in which they will be filed
    D. mend torn papers with cellophane tape

5.____

6. Of the following, the BEST reason for a clerical unit to have its own duplicating machine is that the unit

    A. uses many forms which it must reproduce internally
    B. must make two copies of each piece of incoming mail for a special file
    C. must make seven copies of each piece of outgoing mail
    D. must type 200 envelopes each month for distribution to the same offices

6.____

7. Several offices use the same photocopying machine.
If each office must pay its share of the cost of running this machine, the BEST way of determining how much of this cost should be charged to each of these offices is to

    A. determine the monthly number of photocopies made by each office
    B. determine the monthly number of originals submitted for photocopying by each office
    C. determine the number of times per day each office uses the photocopy machine
    D. divide the total cost of running the photocopy machine by the total number of offices using the machine

7.____

8. Which one of the following would it be BEST to use to indicate that a file folder has been removed from the files for temporary use in another office?
A(n)

    A. cross-reference card   B. tickler file marker
    C. aperture card   D. out guide

8.____

9. Which one of the following is the MOST important objective of filing?

    A. Giving a secretary something to do in her spare time
    B. Making it possible to locate information quickly
    C. Providing a place to store unneeded documents
    D. Keeping extra papers from accumulating on workers' desks

9.____

10. If a check has been made out for an incorrect amount, the BEST action for the writer of the check to take is to

    A. erase the original amount and enter the correct amount
    B. cross out the original amount with a single line and enter the correct amount above it
    C. black out the original amount so that it cannot be read and enter the correct amount above it
    D. write a new check

10.____

11. Which one of the following BEST describes the usual arrangement of a tickler file?

    A. Alphabetical   B. Chronological
    C. Numerical   D. Geographical

11.____

12. Which one of the following is the LEAST desirable filing practice?

    A. Using staples to keep papers together
    B. Filing all material without regard to date
    C. Keeping a record of all materials removed from the files
    D. Writing filing instructions on each paper prior to filing

12.____

13. Assume that one of your duties is to keep records of the office supplies used by your unit for the purpose of ordering new supplies when the old supplies run out. The information that will be of MOST help in letting you know when to reorder supplies is the   13.____

    A. quantity issued   B. quantity received
    C. quantity on hand   D. stock number

Questions 14-19.

DIRECTIONS: Questions 14 through 19 consist of sets of names and addresses. In each question, the name and address in Column II should be an exact copy of the name and address in Column I. If there is:
        a mistake *only* in the name, mark your answer A;
        a mistake *only* in the address, mark your answer B;
        a mistake in *both* name and address, mark your answer C;
        no mistake in *either* name or address, mark your answer D.

SAMPLE QUESTION

Column I
Michael Filbert
456 Reade Street
New York, N.Y. 10013

Column II
Michael Filbert
645 Reade Street
New York, N.Y. 10013

Since there is a mistake only in the address (the street number should be 456 instead of 645), the answer to the sample question is B.

COLUMN I

COLUMN II

14. Esta Wong
    141 West 68 St.
    New York, N.Y. 10023

    Esta Wang
    141 West 68 St.
    New York, N.Y. 10023   14.____

15. Dr. Alberto Grosso
    3475 12th Avenue
    Brooklyn, N.Y. 11218

    Dr. Alberto Grosso
    3475 12th Avenue
    Brooklyn, N.Y. 11218   15.____

16. Mrs. Ruth Bortlas
    482 Theresa Ct.
    Far Rockaway, N.Y. 11691

    Ms. Ruth Bortlas
    482 Theresa Ct.
    Far Rockaway, N.Y. 11169   16.____

17. Mr. and Mrs. Howard Fox
    2301 Sedgwick Ave.
    Bronx, N.Y. 10468

    Mr. and Mrs. Howard Fox
    231 Sedgwick Ave.
    Bronx, N.Y. 10468   17.____

18. Miss Marjorie Black
    223 East 23 Street
    New York, N.Y. 10010

    Miss Margorie Black
    223 East 23 Street
    New York, N.Y. 10010   18.____

19. Michelle Herman
    806 Valley Rd.
    Old Tappan, N.J. 07675

    Michelle Hermann
    806 Valley Dr.
    Old Tappan, N.J. 07675   19.____

Questions 20-25.

DIRECTIONS: Questions 20 through 25 are to be answered SOLELY on the basis of the information in the following passage.

Basic to every office is the need for proper lighting. Inadequate lighting is a familiar cause
of fatigue and serves to create a somewhat dismal atmosphere in the office. One requirement
of proper lighting is that it be of an appropriate intensity. Intensity is measured in foot-candles.
According to the Illuminating Engineering Society of New York, for casual seeing tasks such
as in reception rooms, inactive file rooms, and other service areas, it is recommended that
the amount of light be 30 foot-candles. For ordinary seeing tasks such as reading and work in
active file rooms and in mail rooms, the recommended lighting is 100 foot-candles. For very
difficult seeing tasks such as accounting, transcribing, and business machine use, the recommended lighting is 150 foot-candles.

Lighting intensity is only one requirement. Shadows and glare are to be avoided. For
example, the larger the proportion of a ceiling filled with lighting units, the more glare-free and
comfortable the lighting will be. Natural lighting from windows is not too dependable because
on dark wintry days, windows yield little usable light, and on sunny, summer afternoons, the
glare from windows may be very distracting. Desks should not face the windows. Finally, the
main lighting source ought to be overhead and to the left of the user.

20.   According to the above passage, insufficient light in the office may cause   20.____

A.   glare   B.   shadows
C.   tiredness   D.   distraction

21.   Based on the above passage, which of the following must be considered when planning   21.____
lighting arrangements?
The

A.   amount of natural light present
B.   amount of work to be done
C.   level of difficulty of work to be done
D.   type of activity to be carried out

22.   It can be inferred from the above passage that a well-coordinated lighting scheme is   22.____
LIKELY to result in

A.   greater employee productivity
B.   elimination of light reflection
C.   lower lighting cost
D.   more use of natural light

23.   Of the following, the BEST title for the above passage is   23.____

A.   Characteristics of Light
B.   Light Measurement Devices
C.   Factors to Consider When Planning Lighting Systems
D.   Comfort vs. Cost When Devising Lighting Arrangements

24. According to the above passage, a foot-candle is a measurement of the   24.____

    A. number of bulbs used
    B. strength of the light
    C. contrast between glare and shadow
    D. proportion of the ceiling filled with lighting units

25. According to the above passage, the number of foot-candles of light that would be   25.____
needed to copy figures onto a payroll is _____ foot-candles.

    A. less than 30   B. 30
    C. 100   D. 150

KEY (CORRECT ANSWERS)

1. B	11. B		
2. B	12. B		
3. B	13. C		
4. A	14. A		
5. B	15. D		
6. A	16. C		
7. A	17. B		
8. D	18. A		
9. B	19. C		
10. D	20. C		

21. D
22. A
23. C
24. B
25. D

TEST 2

DIRECTIONS: Each question or incomplete statement is followed by several suggested answers or completions. Select the one that BEST answers the question or completes the statement. *PRINT THE LETTER OF THE CORRECT ANSWER IN THE SPACE AT THE RIGHT.*

1. Assume that a supervisor has three subordinates who perform clerical tasks. One of the employees retires and is replaced by someone who is transferred from another unit in the agency. The transferred employee tells the supervisor that she has worked as a clerical employee for two years and understands clerical operations quite well. The supervisor then assigns the transferred employee to a desk, tells the employee to begin working, and returns to his own desk.
   The supervisor's action in this situation is   1.____

   A. *proper;* experienced clerical employees do not require training when they are transferred to new assignments
   B. *improper;* before the supervisor returns to his desk, he should tell the other two subordinates to watch the transferred employee perform the work
   C. *proper;* if the transferred employee makes any mistakes, she will bring them to the supervisor's attention
   D. *improper;* the supervisor should find out what clerical tasks the transferred employee has performed and give her instruction in those which are new or different

2. Assume that you are falling behind in completing your work assignments and you believe that your workload is too heavy.
   Of the following, the BEST course of action for you to take FIRST is to   2.____

   A. discuss the problem with your supervisor
   B. decide which of your assignments can be postponed
   C. try to get some of your co-workers to help you out
   D. plan to take some of the work home with you in order to catch up

3. Suppose that one of the clerks under your supervision is filling in monthly personnel forms. She asks you to explain a particular personnel regulation which is related to various items on the forms. You are not thoroughly familiar with the regulation.
   Of the following responses you may make, the one which will gain the MOST respect from the clerk and which is generally the MOST advisable is to   3.____

   A. tell the clerk to do the best she can and that you will check her work later
   B. inform the clerk that you are not sure of a correct explanation but suggest a procedure for her to follow
   C. give the clerk a suitable interpretation so that she will think you are familiar with all regulations
   D. tell the clerk that you will have to read the regulation more thoroughly before you can give her an explanation

4. Charging out records until a specified due date, with prompt follow-up if they are not returned, is a   4.____

A. *good* idea; it may prevent the records from being kept needlessly on someone's desk for long periods of time
B. *good* idea; it will indicate the extent of your authority to other departments
C. *poor* idea; the person borrowing the material may make an error because of the pressure put upon him to return the records
D. *poor* idea; other departments will feel that you do not trust them with the records and they will be resentful

Questions 5-9.

DIRECTIONS: Questions 5 through 9 consist of three lines of code letters and numbers. The numbers on each line should correspond with the code letters on the same line in accordance with the table below.

Code Letter	P	L	I	J	B	O	H	U	C	G
Corresponding Number	0	1	2	3	4	5	6	7	8	9

On some of the lines, an error exists in the coding. Compare the letters and numbers in each question carefully. If you find an error or errors on
only *one* of the lines in the question, mark your answer A;
any *two* lines in the question, mark your answer B;
all *three* lines in the question, mark your answer C;
none of the lines in the question, mark your answer D.

SAMPLE QUESTION

JHOILCP   3652180
BICLGUP   4286970
UCIBHLJ   5824613

In the above sample, the first line is correct since each code letter listed has the correct corresponding number. On the second line, an error exists because code letter L should have the number 1 instead of the number 6. On the third line, an error exists because the code letter U should have the number 7 instead of the number 5. Since there are errors on two of the three lines, the correct answer is B.

5. BULJCIP   4713920   5.____
   HIGPOUL   6290571
   OCUHJBI   5876342

6. CUBLOIJ   8741023   6.____
   LCLGCLB   1818914
   JPUHIOC   3076158

7. OIJGCBPO   52398405   7.____
   UHPBLIOP   76041250
   CLUIPGPC   81720908

8. BPCOUOJI   40875732   8.____
    UOHCIPLB   75682014
    GLHUUCBJ   92677843

9. HOIOHJLH   65256361   9.____
    IOJJHHBP   25536640
    OJHBJOPI   53642502

Questions 10-13.

DIRECTIONS: Questions 10 through 13 are to be answered SOLELY on the basis of the information given in the following passage.

The mental attitude of the employee toward safety is exceedingly important in preventing accidents. All efforts designed to keep safety on the employee's mind and to keep accident prevention a live subject in the office will help substantially in a safety program. Although it may seem strange, it is common for people to be careless. Therefore, safety education is a continuous process.

Safety rules should be explained, and the reasons for their rigid enforcement should be given to employees. Telling employees to be careful or giving similar general safety warnings and slogans is probably of little value. Employees should be informed of basic safety fundamentals. This can be done through staff meetings, informal suggestions to employees, movies, and safety instruction cards. Safety instruction cards provide the employees with specific suggestions about safety and serve as a series of timely reminders helping to keep safety on the minds of employees. Pictures, posters, and cartoon sketches on bulletin boards that are located in areas continually used by employees arouse the employees' interest in safety. It is usually good to supplement this type of safety promotion with intensive individual follow-up.

10. The above passage implies that the LEAST effective of the following safety measures is   10.____

    A.   rigid enforcement of safety rules
    B.   getting employees to think in terms of safety
    C.   elimination of unsafe conditions in the office
    D.   telling employees to stay alert at all times

11. The reason given by the passage for maintaining ongoing safety education is that   11.____

    A.   people are often careless
    B.   office tasks are often dangerous
    C.   the value of safety slogans increases with repetition
    D.   safety rules change frequently

12. Which one of the following safety aids is MOST likely to be preferred by the passage?   12.____
    A

    A.   cartoon of a man tripping over a carton and yelling, *Keep aisles clear!*
    B.   poster with a large number one and a caption saying, *Safety First*
    C.   photograph of a very neatly arranged office
    D.   large sign with the word *THINK* in capital letters

13. Of the following, the BEST title for the above passage is 13.____
   A. Basic Safety Fundamentals
   B. Enforcing Safety Among Careless Employees
   C. Attitudes Toward Safety
   D. Making Employees Aware of Safety

Questions 14-21.

DIRECTIONS: Questions 14 through 21 are to be answered SOLELY on the basis of the information and the chart given below.

The following chart shows expenses in five selected categories for a one-year period, expressed as percentages of these same expenses during the previous year. The chart compares two different offices. In Office T (represented by), a cost reduction program has been tested for the past year. The other office, Office Q (represented by), served as a control, in that no special effort was made' to reduce costs during the past year.

RESULTS OF OFFICE COST REDUCTION PROGRAM
Expenses of Test and Control Groups for 2016
Expressed as Percentages of Same Expenses for 2015

Test Group (Office T)   Control Group (Office Q)

14. In Office T, which category of expense showed the greatest percentage REDUCTION from 2015 to 2016? 14.____

   A. Telephone   B. Office Supplies
   C. Postage & Mailing D. Overtime

15. In which expense category did Office T show the BEST results in percentage terms when compared to Office Q? 15.____

   A. Telephone   B. Office Supplies
   C. Postage & Mailing D. Overtime

16. According to the above chart, the cost reduction program was LEAST effective for the   16.____
    expense category of

    A. Office Supplies   B. Postage & Mailing
    C. Equipment Repair   D. Overtime

17. Office T's telephone costs went down during 2016 by approximately how many percent-   17.____
    age points?

    A. 15   B. 20   C. 85   D. 105

18. Which of the following changes occurred in expenses for Office Supplies in Office Q in   18.____
    the year 2016 as compared with the year 2015?
    They

    A. increased by more than 100%
    B. remained the same
    C. decreased by a few percentage points
    D. increased by a few percentage points

19. For which of the following expense categories do the results in Office T and the results in   19.____
    Office Q differ MOST NEARLY by 10 percentage points?

    A. Telephone   B. Postage & Mailing
    C. Equipment Repair   D. Overtime

20. In which expense category did Office Q's costs show the GREATEST percentage   20.____
    increase in 2016?

    A. Telephone   B. Office Supplies
    C. Postage & Mailing   D. Equipment Repair

21. In Office T, by approximately what percentage did overtime expense change during the   21.____
    past year?
    It

    A. *increased* by 15%   B. *increased* by 75%
    C. *decreased* by 10%   D. *decreased* by 25%

22. In a particular agency, there were 160 accidents in 2007. Of these accidents, 75% were   22.____
    due to unsafe acts and the rest were due to unsafe conditions. In the following year, a
    special safety program was established. The number of accidents in 2009 due to unsafe
    acts was reduced to 35% of what it had been in 2007.
    How many accidents due to unsafe acts were there in 2009?

    A. 20   B. 36   C. 42   D. 56

23. At the end of every month, the petty cash fund of Agency A is reimbursed for payments   23.____
    made from the fund during the month. During the month of February, the amounts paid
    from the fund were entered on receipts as follows: 10 bus fares of 35¢ each and one taxi
    fare of $3.50.
    At the end of the month, the money left in the fund was in the following denominations:
    15 one dollar bills, 4 quarters, 10 dimes, and 20 nickels.
    If the petty cash fund is reduced by 20% for the following month, how much money will
    there be available in the petty cash fund for March?

    A. $11.00   B. $20.00   C. $21.50   D. $25.00

24. The one of the following records which it would be MOST advisable to keep in alphabeti-   24._____
    cal order is a

    A. continuous listing of phone messages, including time and caller, for your supervi-
       sor
    B. listing of individuals currently employed by your agency in a particular title
    C. record of purchases paid for by the petty cash fund
    D. dated record of employees who have borrowed material from the files in your office

25. Assume that you have been asked to copy by hand a column of numbers with two deci-   25._____
    mal places from one record to another. Each number consists of three, four, and five dig-
    its.
    In order to copy them quickly and accurately, you should copy

    A. each number exactly, making sure that the column of digits farthest to the right is in
       a straight line and all other columns are lined up
    B. the column of digits farthest to the right and then copy the next column of digits
       moving from right to left
    C. the column of digits farthest to the left and then copy the next column of digits mov-
       ing from left to right
    D. the digits to the right of each decimal point and then copy the digits to the left of
       each decimal point

KEY (CORRECT ANSWERS)

1.	D	11.	A
2.	A	12.	A
3.	D	13.	D
4.	A	14.	D
5.	A	15.	A
6.	C	16.	C
7.	D	17.	A
8.	B	18.	D
9.	C	19.	B
10.	D	20.	C

21.	D
22.	C
23.	B
24.	B
25.	A

RECORD KEEPING
EXAMINATION SECTION
TEST 1

DIRECTIONS: Each question or incomplete statement is followed by several suggested answers or completions. Select the one that BEST answers the question or completes the statement. *PRINT THE LETTER OF THE CORRECT ANSWER IN THE SPACE AT THE RIGHT.*

Questions 1-15.

DIRECTIONS: Questions 1 through 15 are to be answered on the basis of the following list of company names below. Arrange a file alphabetically, word-by-word, disregarding punctuation, conjunctions, and apostrophes. Then answer the questions.

A Bee C Reading Materials
ABCO Parts
A Better Course for Test Preparation
AAA Auto Parts Co.
A-Z Auto Parts, Inc.
Aabar Books
Abbey, Joanne
Boman-Sylvan Law Firm
BMW Autowerks
C Q Service Company
Chappell-Murray, Inc.
E&E Life Insurance
Emcrisco
Gigi Arts
Gordon, Jon & Associates
SOS Plumbing
Schmidt, J.B. Co.

1.   Which of these files should appear FIRST?   1._____

    A.   ABCO Parts
    B.   A Bee C Reading Materials
    C.   A Better Course for Test Preparation
    D.   AAA Auto Parts Co.

2.   Which of these files should appear SECOND?   2._____

    A.   A-Z Auto Parts, Inc.
    B.   A Bee C Reading Materials
    C.   A Better Course for Test Preparation
    D.   AAA Auto Parts Co.

3.   Which of these files should appear THIRD?   3._____

    A.   ABCO Parts
    B.   A Bee C Reading Materials
    C.   Aabar Books
    D.   AAA Auto Parts Co.

4. Which of these files should appear FOURTH?   4.____

    A. Aabar Books
    B. ABCO Parts
    C. Abbey, Joanne
    D. AAA Auto Parts Co.

5. Which of these files should appear LAST?   5.____

    A. Gordon, Jon & Associates
    B. Gigi Arts
    C. Schmidt, J.B. Co.
    D. SOS Plumbing

6. Which of these files should appear between A-Z Auto Parts, Inc. and Abbey, Joanne?   6.____

    A. A Bee C Reading Materials
    B. AAA Auto Parts Co.
    C. ABCO Parts
    D. A Better Course for Test Preparation

7. Which of these files should appear between ABCO Parts and Aabar Books?   7.____

    A. A Bee C Reading Materials
    B. Abbey, Joanne
    C. Aabar Books
    D. A-Z Auto Parts

8. Which of these files should appear between Abbey, Joanne and Boman-Sylvan Law Firm?   8.____

    A. A Better Course for Test Preparation
    B. BMW Autowerks
    C. Chappell-Murray, Inc.
    D. Aabar Books

9. Which of these files should appear between Abbey, Joanne and C Q Service?   9.____

    A. A-Z Auto Parts,Inc.   B. BMW Autowerks
    C. Choices A and B   D. Chappell-Murray, Inc.

10. Which of these files should appear between C Q Service Company and Emcrisco?   10.____

    A. Chappell-Murray, Inc.   B. E&E Life Insurance
    C. Gigi Arts   D. Choices A and B

11. Which of these files should NOT appear between C Q Service Company and E&E Life Insurance?   11.____

    A. Gordon, Jon & Associates
    B. Emcrisco
    C. Gigi Arts
    D. All of the above

12. Which of these files should appear between Chappell-Murray Inc., and Gigi Arts? 12.____

    A. CQ Service Inc. E&E Life Insurance, and Emcrisco
    B. Emcrisco, E&E Life Insurance, and Gordon, Jon & Associates
    C. E&E Life Insurance and Emcrisco
    D. Emcrisco and Gordon, Jon & Associates

13. Which of these files should appear between Gordon, Jon & Associates and SOS Plumbing? 13.____

    A. Gigi Arts   B. Schmidt, J.B. Co.
    C. Choices A and B   D. None of the above

14. Each of the choices lists the four files in their proper alphabetical order except 14.____

    A. E&E Life Insurance; Gigi Arts; Gordon, Jon & Associates; SOS Plumbing
    B. E&E Life Insurance; Emcrisco; Gigi Arts; SOS Plumbing
    C. Emcrisco; Gordon, Jon & Associates; SOS Plumbing; Schmidt, J.B. Co.
    D. Emcrisco; Gigi Arts; Gordon, Jon & Associates; SOS Plumbing

15. Which of the choices lists the four files in their proper alphabetical order? 15.____

    A. Gigi Arts; Gordon, Jon & Associates; SOS Plumbing; Schmidt, J.B. Co.
    B. Gordon, Jon & Associates; Gigi Arts; Schmidt, J.B. Co.; SOS Plumbing
    C. Gordon, Jon & Associates; Gigi Arts; SOS Plumbing; Schmidt, J.B. Co.
    D. Gigi Arts; Gordon, Jon & Associates; Schmidt, J.B. Co.; SOS Plumbing

16. The alphabetical filing order of two businesses with identical names is determined by the 16.____

    A. length of time each business has been operating
    B. addresses of the businesses
    C. last name of the company president
    D. none of the above

17. In an alphabetical filing system, if a business name includes a number, it should be 17.____

    A. disregarded
    B. considered a number and placed at the end of an alphabetical section
    C. treated as though it were written in words and alphabetized accordingly
    D. considered a number and placed at the beginning of an alphabetical section

18. If a business name includes a contraction (such as *don't* or *it's*), how should that word be treated in an alphabetical filing system? 18.____

    A. Divide the word into its separate parts and treat it as two words.
    B. Ignore the letters that come after the apostrophe.
    C. Ignore the word that contains the contraction.
    D. Ignore the apostrophe and consider all letters in the contraction.

19. In what order should the parts of an address be considered when using an alphabetical filing system? 19.____

    A. City or town; state; street name; house or building number
    B. State; city or town; street name; house or building number
    C. House or building number; street name; city or town; state
    D. Street name; city or town; state

20. A business record should be cross-referenced when a(n)   20.____

    A. organization is known by an abbreviated name
    B. business has a name change because of a sale, incorporation, or other reason
    C. business is known by a *coined* or common name which differs from a dictionary spelling
    D. all of the above

21. A geographical filing system is MOST effective when   21.____

    A. location is more important than name
    B. many names or titles sound alike
    C. dealing with companies who have offices all over the world
    D. filing personal and business files

Questions 22-25.

DIRECTIONS: Questions 22 through 25 are to be answered on the basis of the list of items below, which are to be filed geographically. Organize the items geographically and then answer the questions.
    1. University Press at Berkeley, U.S.
    2. Maria Sanchez, Mexico City, Mexico
    3. Great Expectations Ltd. in London, England
    4. Justice League, Cape Town, South Africa, Africa
    5. Crown Pearls Ltd. in London, England
    6. Joseph Prasad in London, England

22. Which of the following arrangements of the items is composed according to the policy of: 22.____
Continent, Country, City, Firm or Individual Name?

    A. 5, 3, 4, 6, 2, 1   B. 4, 5, 3, 6, 2, 1
    C. 1, 4, 5, 3, 6, 2   D. 4, 5, 3, 6, 1, 2

23. Which of the following files is arranged according to the policy of: *Continent, Country,*   23.____
City, Firm or Individual Name?

    A. South Africa. Africa. Cape Town. Justice League
    B. Mexico. Mexico City, Maria Sanchez
    C. North America. United States. Berkeley. University Press
    D. England. Europe. London. Prasad, Joseph

24. Which of the following arrangements of the items is composed according to the policy of: 24.____
Country, City, Firm or Individual Name?

    A. 5, 6, 3, 2, 4, 1   B. 1, 5, 6, 3, 2, 4
    C. 6, 5, 3, 2, 4, 1   D. 5, 3, 6, 2, 4, 1

25. Which of the following files is arranged according to a policy of: *Country, City, Firm or*   25.____
Individual Name?

    A. England. London. Crown Pearls Ltd.
    B. North America. United States. Berkeley. University Press
    C. Africa. Cape Town. Justice League
    D. Mexico City. Mexico. Maria Sanchez

26. Under which of the following circumstances would a phonetic filing system be MOST effective?   26.____

    A. When the person in charge of filing can't spell very well
    B. With large files with names that sound alike
    C. With large files with names that are spelled alike
    D. All of the above

Questions 27-29.

DIRECTIONS: Questions 27 through 29 are to be answered on the basis of the following list of numerical files.
    1. 391-023-100
    2. 361-132-170
    3. 385-732-200
    4. 381-432-150
    5. 391-632-387
    6. 361-423-303
    7. 391-123-271

27. Which of the following arrangements of the files follows a consecutive-digit system?   27.____

    A. 2, 3, 4, 1   B. 1, 5, 7, 3
    C. 2, 4, 3, 1   D. 3, 1, 5, 7

28. Which of the following arrangements follows a terminal-digit system?   28.____

    A. 1, 7, 2, 4, 3   B. 2, 1, 4, 5, 7
    C. 7, 6, 5, 4, 3   D. 1, 4, 2, 3, 7

29. Which of the following lists follows a middle-digit system?   29.____

    A. 1, 7, 2, 6, 4, 5, 3   B. 1, 2, 7, 4, 6, 5, 3
    C. 7, 2, 1, 3, 5, 6, 4   D. 7, 1, 2, 4, 6, 5, 3

Questions 30-31.

DIRECTIONS: Questions 30 and 31 are to be answered on the basis of the following information.
    1. Reconfirm Laura Bates appointment with James Caldecort on December 12 at 9:30 A.M.
    2. Laurence Kinder contact Julia Lucas on August 3 and set up a meeting for week of September 23 at 4 P.M.
    3. John Lutz contact Larry Waverly on August 3 and set up appointment for September 23 at 9:30 A.M.
    4. Call for tickets for Gerry Stanton August 21 for New Jersey on September 23, flight 143 at 4:43 P.M.

30. A chronological file for the above information would be   30.____

    A. 4, 3, 2, 1   B. 3, 2, 4, 1
    C. 4, 2, 3, 1   D. 3, 1, 2, 4

31. Using the above information, a chronological file for the date of September 23 would be   31.____

    A. 2, 3, 4   B. 3, 1, 4   C. 3, 2, 4   D. 4, 3, 2

Questions 32-34.

DIRECTIONS: Questions 32 through 34 are to be answered on the basis of the following information.
1. Call Roger Epstein, Ashoke Naipaul, Jon Anderson, and Sarah Washington on April 19 at 1:00 P.M. to set up meeting with Alika D'Ornay for June 6 in New York.
2. Call Martin Ames before noon on April 19 to confirm afternoon meeting with Bob Greenwood on April 20th
3. Set up meeting room at noon for 2:30 P.M. meeting on April 19th;
4. Ashley Stanton contact Bob Greenwood at 9:00 A.M. on April 20 and set up meeting for June 6 at 8:30 A.M.
5. Carol Guiland contact Shelby Van Ness during afternoon of April 20 and set up meeting for June 6 at 10:00 A.M.
6. Call airline and reserve tickets on June 6 for Roger Epstein trip *to* Denver on July 8
7. Meeting at 2:30 P.M. on April 19th

32. A chronological file for all of the above information would be   32.____

    A. 2, 1, 3, 7, 5, 4, 6   B. 3, 7, 2, 1, 4, 5, 6
    C. 3, 7, 1, 2, 5, 4, 6   D. 2, 3, 1, 7, 4, 5, 6

33. A chronological file for the date of April 19th would be   33.____

    A. 2, 3, 7, 1   B. 2, 3, 1, 7
    C. 7, 1, 3, 2   D. 3, 7, 1, 2

34. Add the following information to the file, and then create a chronological file for April 20th: 34.____
8. April 20: 3:00 P.M. meeting between Bob Greenwood and Martin Ames.

    A. 4, 5, 8   B. 4, 8, 5   C. 8, 5, 4   D. 5, 4, 8

35. The PRIMARY advantage of computer records filing over a manual system is   35.____

    A. speed of retrieval   B. accuracy
    C. cost   D. potential file loss

KEY (CORRECT ANSWERS)

1.	B		16.	B
2.	C		17.	C
3.	D		18.	D
4.	A		19.	A
5.	D		20.	D
6.	C		21.	A
7.	B		22.	B
8.	B		23.	C
9.	C		24.	D
10.	D		25.	A
11.	D		26.	B
12.	C		27.	C
13.	B		28.	D
14.	C		29.	A
15.	D		30.	B

31.	C
32.	D
33.	B
34.	A
35.	A

CLERICAL ABILITIES

EXAMINATION SECTION
TEST 1

DIRECTIONS: Each question or incomplete statement is followed by several suggested answers or completions. Select the one that BEST answers the question or completes the statement. *PRINT THE LETTER OF THE CORRECT ANSWER IN THE SPACE AT THE RIGHT.*

Questions 1-4.

DIRECTIONS: Questions 1 through 4 are to be answered on the basis of the information given below.

The most commonly used filing system and the one that is easiest to learn is alphabetical filing. This involves putting records in an A to Z order, according to the letters of the alphabet. The name of a person is filed by using the following order: first, the surname or last name; second, the first name; third, the middle name or middle initial. For example, *Henry C. Young* is filed under *Y* and thereafter under *Young, Henry C.* The name of a company is filed in the same way. For example, *Long Cabinet Co.* is filed under *L*, while *John T. Long Cabinet Co.* is filed under *L* and thereafter under *Long., John T. Cabinet Co.*

1. The one of the following which lists the names of persons in the CORRECT alphabetical order is:

    A. Mary Carrie, Helen Carrol, James Carson, John Carter
    B. James Carson, Mary Carrie, John Carter, Helen Carrol
    C. Helen Carrol, James Carson, John Carter, Mary Carrie
    D. John Carter, Helen Carrol, Mary Carrie, James Carson

1.____

2. The one of the following which lists the names of persons in the CORRECT alphabetical order is:

    A. Jones, John C.; Jones, John A.; Jones, John P.; Jones, John K.
    B. Jones, John P.; Jones, John K.; Jones, John C.; Jones, John A.
    C. Jones, John A.; Jones, John C.; Jones, John K.; Jones, John P.
    D. Jones, John K.; Jones, John C.; Jones, John A.; Jones, John P.

2.____

3. The one of the following which lists the names of the companies in the CORRECT alphabetical order is:

    A. Blane Co., Blake Co., Block Co., Blear Co.
    B. Blake Co., Blane Co., Blear Co., Block Co.
    C. Block Co., Blear Co., Blane Co., Blake Co.
    D. Blear Co., Blake Co., Blane Co., Block Co.

3.____

4. You are to return to the file an index card on *Barry C. Wayne Materials and Supplies Co.* Of the following, the CORRECT alphabetical group that you should return the index card to is

    A. A to G   B. H to M   C. N to S   D. T to Z

4.____

Questions 5-10.

DIRECTIONS: In each of Questions 5 through 10, the names of four people are given. For each question, choose as your answer the one of the four names given which should be filed FIRST according to the usual system of alphabetical filing of names, as described in the following paragraph.

In filing names, you must start with the last name. Names are filed in order of the first letter of the last name, then the second letter, etc. Therefore, BAILY would be filed before BROWN, which would be filed before COLT. A name with fewer letters of the same type comes first; i.e., Smith before Smithe. If the last names are the same, the names are filed alphabetically by the first name. If the first name is an initial, a name with an initial would come before a first name that starts with the same letter as the initial. Therefore, I. BROWN would come before IRA BROWN. Finally, if both last name and first name are the same, the name would be filed alphabetically by the middle name, once again an initial coming before a middle name which starts with the same letter as the initial. If there is no middle name at all, the name would come before those with middle initials or names.

Sample Question: A.   Lester Daniels
                   B.   William Dancer
                   C.   Nathan Danzig
                   D.   Dan Lester

The last names beginning with D are filed before the last name beginning with L. Since DANIELS, DANCER, and DANZIG all begin with the same three letters, you must look at the fourth letter of the last name to determine which name should be filed first. C comes before I or Z in the alphabet, so DANCER is filed before DANIELS or DANZIG. Therefore, the answer to the above sample question is B.

5.   A.   Scott Biala   5._____
     B.   Mary Byala
     C.   Martin Baylor
     D.   Francis Bauer

6.   A.   Howard J. Black   6._____
     B.   Howard Black
     C.   J. Howard Black
     D.   John H. Black

7.   A.   Theodora Garth Kingston   7._____
     B.   Theadore Barth Kingston
     C.   Thomas Kingston
     D.   Thomas T. Kingston

8.   A.   Paulette Mary Huerta   8._____
     B.   Paul M. Huerta
     C.   Paulette L. Huerta
     D.   Peter A. Huerta

9. A. Martha Hunt Morgan   9._____
   B. Martin Hunt Morgan
   C. Mary H. Morgan
   D. Martine H. Morgan

10. A. James T. Meerschaum   10._____
    B. James M. Mershum
    C. James F. Mearshaum
    D. James N. Meshum

Questions 11-14.

DIRECTIONS: Questions 11 through 14 are to be answered SOLELY on the basis of the following information.

You are required to file various documents in file drawers which are labeled according to the following pattern:

DOCUMENTS

MEMOS		LETTERS	
File	Subject	File	Subject
84PM1 - (A-L)		84PC1 - (A-L)	
84PM2 - (M-Z)		84PC2 - (M-Z)	

REPORTS		INQUIRIES	
File	Subject	File	Subject
84PR1 - (A-L)		84PQ1 - (A-L)	
84PR2 - (M-Z)		84PQ2 - (M-Z)	

11. A letter dealing with a burglary should be filed in the drawer labeled   11._____

     A. 84PM1   B. 84PC1   C. 84PR1   D. 84PQ2

12. A report on Statistics should be found in the drawer labeled   12._____

     A. 84PM1   B. 84PC2   C. 84PR2   D. 84PQ2

13. An inquiry is received about parade permit procedures. It should be filed in the drawer labeled   13._____

     A. 84PM2   B. 84PC1   C. 84PR1   D. 84PQ2

14. A police officer has a question about a robbery report you filed.
    You should pull this file from the drawer labeled   14._____

     A. 84PM1   B. 84PM2   C. 84PR1   D. 84PR2

Questions 15-22.

DIRECTIONS: Each of Questions 15 through 22 consists of four or six numbered names. For each question, choose the option (A, B, C, or D) which indicates the order in which the names should be filed in accordance with the following filing instructions:
- File alphabetically according to last name, then first name, then middle initial.
- File according to each successive letter within a name.

- When comparing two names in which, the letters in the longer name are identical to the corresponding letters in the shorter name, the shorter name is filed first.
- When the last names are the same, initials are always filed before names beginning with the same letter.

15.   I.   Ralph Robinson   15.____
            II. Alfred Ross
           III. Luis Robles
           IV. James Roberts

The CORRECT filing sequence for the above names should be

A. IV, II, I, III   B. I, IV, III, II
C. III, IV, I, II   D. IV, I, III, II

16.   I.   Irwin Goodwin   16.____
            II. Inez Gonzalez
           III. Irene Goodman
           IV. Ira S. Goodwin
           V. Ruth I. Goldstein
          VI. M.B. Goodman

The CORRECT filing sequence for the above names should be

A. V, II, I, IV, III, VI   B. V, II, VI, III, IV, I
C. V, II, III, VI, IV, I   D. V, II, III, VI, I, IV

17.   I.   George Allan   17.____
            II. Gregory Allen
           III. Gary Allen
           IV. George Allen

The CORRECT filing sequence for the above names should be

A. IV, III, I, II   B. I, IV, II, III
C. III, IV, I, II   D. I, III, IV, II

18.   I.   Simon Kauffman   18.____
            II. Leo Kaufman
           III. Robert Kaufmann
           IV. Paul Kauffmann

The CORRECT filing sequence for the above names should be

A. I, IV, II, III   B. II, IV, III, I
C. III, II, IV, I   D. I, II, III, IV

19.   I.   Roberta Williams   19.____
            II. Robin Wilson
           III. Roberta Wilson
           IV. Robin Williams

The CORRECT filing sequence for the above names should be

A. III, II, IV, I   B. I, IV, III, II
C. I, II, III, IV   D. III, I, II, IV

20.   I.   Lawrence Shultz   20.____
           II.   Albert Schultz
         III.   Theodore Schwartz
         IV.   Thomas Schwarz
          V.   Alvin Schultz
         VI.   Leonard Shultz

The CORRECT filing sequence for the above names should be

  A. II, V, III, IV, I, VI   B. IV, III, V, I, II, VI
  C. II, V, I, VI, III, IV   D. I, VI, II, V, III, IV

21.   I.   McArdle   21.____
           II.   Mayer
         III.   Maletz
         IV.   McNiff
          V.   Meyer
         VI.   MacMahon

The CORRECT filing sequence for the above names should be

  A. I, IV, VI, III, II, V   B. II, I, IV, VI, III, V
  C. VI, III, II, I, IV, V   D. VI, III, II, V, I, IV

22.   I.   Jack E. Johnson   22.____
           II.   R.H. Jackson
         III.   Bertha Jackson
         IV.   J.T. Johnson
          V.   Ann Johns
         VI.   John Jacobs

The CORRECT filing sequence for the above names should be

  A. II, III, VI, V, IV, I   B. III, II, VI, V, IV, I
  C. VI, II, III, I, V, IV   D. III, II, VI, IV, V, I

Questions 23-30.

DIRECTIONS: The code table below shows 10 letters with matching numbers. For each question, there are three sets of letters. Each set of letters is followed by a set of numbers which may or may not match their correct letter according to the code table. For each question, check all three sets of letters and numbers and mark your answer:
      A.   if no pairs are correctly matched
      B.   if only one pair is correctly matched
      C.   if only two pairs are correctly matched
      D.   if all three pairs are correctly matched

CODE TABLE

T	M	V	D	S	P	R	G	B	H
1	2	3	4	5	6	7	8	9	0

Sample Question: TMVDSP - 123456
                        RGBHTM - 789011
                        DSPRGB - 256789

In the sample question above, the first set of numbers correctly matches its set of letters. But the second and third pairs contain mistakes. In the second pair, M is incorrectly matched with number 1. According to the code table, letter M should be correctly matched with number 2. In the third pair, the letter D is incorrectly matched with number 2. According to the code table, letter D should be correctly matched with number 4. Since only one of the pairs is correctly matched, the answer to this sample question is B.

23. RSBMRM 759262
    GDSRVH 845730
    VDBRTM 349713

23._____

24. TGVSDR 183247
    SMHRDP 520647
    TRMHSR 172057

24._____

25. DSPRGM 456782
    MVDBHT 234902
    HPMDBT 062491

25._____

26. BVPTRD 936184
    GDPHMB 807029
    GMRHMV 827032

26._____

27. MGVRSH 283750
    TRDMBS 174295
    SPRMGV 567283

27._____

28. SGBSDM 489542
    MGHPTM 290612
    MPBMHT 269301

28._____

29. TDPBHM 146902
    VPBMRS 369275
    GDMBHM 842902

29._____

30. MVPTBV 236194
    PDRTMB 647128
    BGTMSM 981232

30._____

KEY (CORRECT ANSWERS)

1.	A	11.	B	21.	C
2.	C	12.	C	22.	B
3.	B	13.	D	23.	B
4.	D	14.	D	24.	B
5.	D	15.	D	25.	C
6.	B	16.	C	26.	A
7.	B	17.	D	27.	D
8.	B	18.	A	28.	A
9.	A	19.	B	29.	D
10.	C	20.	A	30.	A

TEST 2

DIRECTIONS: Each question or incomplete statement is followed by several suggested answers or completions. Select the one that BEST answers the question or completes the statement. *PRINT THE LETTER OF THE CORRECT ANSWER IN THE SPACE AT THE RIGHT.*

Questions 1-10.

DIRECTIONS: Questions 1 through 10 each consists of two columns, each containing four lines of names, numbers and/or addresses. For each question, compare the lines in Column I with the lines in Column II to see if they match exactly, and mark your answer A, B, C, or D, according to the following instructions:
- A.   all four lines match exactly
- B.   only three lines match exactly
- C.   only two lines match exactly
- D.   only one line matches exactly

	COLUMN I	COLUMN II	
1.	I. Earl Hodgson II. 1409870 III. Shore Ave. IV. Macon Rd.	Earl Hodgson 1408970 Schore Ave. Macon Rd.	1.____
2.	I. 9671485 II. 470 Astor Court III. Halprin, Phillip IV. Frank D. Poliseo	9671485 470 Astor Court Halperin, Phillip Frank D. Poliseo	2.____
3.	I. Tandem Associates II. 144-17 Northern Blvd. III. Alberta Forchi IV. Kings Park, NY 10751	Tandom Associates 144-17 Northern Blvd. Albert Forchi Kings Point, NY 10751	3.____
4.	I. Bertha C. McCormack II. Clayton, MO. III. 976-4242 IV. New City, NY 10951	Bertha C. McCormack Clayton, MO. 976-4242 New City, NY 10951	4.____
5.	I. George C. Morill II. Columbia, SC 29201 III. Louis Ingham IV. 3406 Forest Ave.	George C. Morrill Columbia, SD 29201 Louis Ingham 3406 Forest Ave.	5.____
6.	I. 506 S. Elliott Pl. II. Herbert Hall III. 4712 Rockaway Pkway IV. 169 E. 7 St.	506 S. Elliott Pl. Hurbert Hall 4712 Rockaway Pkway 169 E. 7 St.	6.____

	COLUMN I	COLUMN II	
7.	I. 345 Park Ave.	345 Park Pl.	7.____
	II. Colman Oven Corp.	Coleman Oven Corp.	
	III. Robert Conte	Robert Conti	
	IV. 6179846	6179846	
8.	I. Grigori Schierber	Grigori Schierber	8.____
	II. Des Moines, Iowa	Des Moines, Iowa	
	III. Gouverneur Hospital	Gouverneur Hospital	
	IV. 91-35 Cresskill Pl.	91-35 Cresskill Pl.	
9.	I. Jeffery Janssen	Jeffrey Janssen	9.____
	II. 8041071	8041071	
	III. 40 Rockefeller Plaza	40 Rockafeller Plaza	
	IV. 407 6 St.	406 7 St.	
10.	I. 5971996	5871996	10.____
	II. 3113 Knickerbocker Ave.	3113 Knickerbocker Ave.	
	III. 8434 Boston Post Rd.	8424 Boston Post Rd.	
	IV. Penn Station	Penn Station	

Questions 11-14.

DIRECTIONS: Questions 11 through 14 are to be answered by looking at the four groups of names and addresses listed below (I, II, III, and IV) and then finding out the number of groups that have their corresponding numbered lines exactly the same.

	GROUP I	GROUP II
Line 1.	Richmond General Hospital	Richman General Hospital
Line 2.	Geriatric Clinic	Geriatric Clinic
Line 3.	3975 Paerdegat St.	3975 Peardegat St.
Line 4	Loudonville, New York 11538	Londonville, New York 11538

	GROUP III	GROUP IV
Line 1.	Richmond General Hospital	Richmend General Hospital
Line 2.	Geriatric Clinic	Geriatric Clinic
Line 3.	3795 Paerdegat St.	3975 Paerdegat St.
Line 4.	Loudonville, New York 11358	Loudonville, New York 11538

11. In how many groups is line one exactly the same?   11.____

    A. Two   B. Three   C. Four   D. None

12. In how many groups is line two exactly the same?   12.____

    A. Two   B. Three   C. Four   D. None

13. In how many groups is line three exactly the same?   13.____

    A. Two   B. Three   C. Four   D. None

14. In how many groups is line four exactly the same?   14._____

    A. Two   B. Three   C. Four   D. None

Questions 15-18.

DIRECTIONS: Each of Questions 15 through 18 has two lists of names and addresses. Each list contains three sets of names and addresses. Check each of the three sets in the list on the right to see if they are the same as the corresponding set in the list on the left. Mark your answers:

    A. if none of the sets in the right list are the same as those in the left list
    B. if only one of the sets in the right list is the same as those in the left list
    C. if only two of the sets in the right list are the same as those in the left list
    D. if all three sets in the right list are the same as those in the left list

15.
Mary T. Berlinger	Mary T. Berlinger	15._____
2351 Hampton St.	2351 Hampton St.	
Monsey, N.Y. 20117	Monsey, N.Y. 20117	
Eduardo Benes	Eduardo Benes	
473 Kingston Avenue	473 Kingston Avenue	
Central Islip, N.Y. 11734	Central Islip, N.Y. 11734	
Alan Carrington Fuchs	Alan Carrington Fuchs	
17 Gnarled Hollow Road	17 Gnarled Hollow Road	
Los Angeles, CA 91635	Los Angeles, CA 91685	

16.
David John Jacobson	David John Jacobson	16._____
178 35 St. Apt. 4C	178 53 St. Apt. 4C	
New York, N.Y. 00927	New York, N.Y. 00927	
Ann-Marie Calonella	Ann-Marie Calonella	
7243 South Ridge Blvd.	7243 South Ridge Blvd.	
Bakersfield, CA 96714	Bakersfield, CA 96714	
Pauline M. Thompson	Pauline M. Thomson	
872 Linden Ave.	872 Linden Ave.	
Houston, Texas 70321	Houston, Texas 70321	

17.
Chester LeRoy Masterton	Chester LeRoy Masterson	17._____
152 Lacy Rd.	152 Lacy Rd.	
Kankakee, Ill. 54532	Kankakee, Ill. 54532	
William Maloney	William Maloney	
S. LaCrosse Pla.	S. LaCross Pla.	
Wausau, Wisconsin 52146	Wausau, Wisconsin 52146	
Cynthia V. Barnes	Cynthia V. Barnes	
16 Pines Rd.	16 Pines Rd.	
Greenpoint, Miss. 20376	Greenpoint, Miss. 20376	

18.   Marcel Jean Frontenac   Marcel Jean Frontenac   18._____
            8 Burton On The Water   6 Burton On The Water
            Calender, Me. 01471   Calender, Me. 01471

            J. Scott Marsden   J. Scott Marsden
            174 S. Tipton St.   174 Tipton St.
            Cleveland, Ohio   Cleveland, Ohio

            Lawrence T. Haney   Lawrence T. Haney
            171 McDonough St.   171 McDonough St.
            Decatur, Ga. 31304   Decatur, Ga. 31304

Questions 19-26.

DIRECTIONS: Each of Questions 19 through 26 has two lists of numbers. Each list contains three sets of numbers. Check each of the three sets in the list on the right to see if they are the same as the corresponding set in the list on the left. Mark your answers:

      A.   if none of the sets in the right list are the same as those in the left list
      B.   if only one of the sets in the right list is the same as those in the left list
      C.   if only two of the sets in the right list are the same as those in the left list
      D.   if all three sets in the right list are the same as those in the left list

19.   7354183476   7354983476   19._____
      4474747744   4474747774
      57914302311   57914302311

20.   7143592185   7143892185   20._____
      8344517699   8344518699
      9178531263   9178531263

21.   2572114731   257214731   21._____
      8806835476   8806835476
      8255831246   8255831246

22.   331476853821   331476858621   22._____
      6976658532996   6976655832996
      3766042113715   3766042113745

23.   8806663315   8806663315   23._____
      74477138449   74477138449
      211756663666   211756663666

24.   990006966996   99000696996   24._____
      53022219743   53022219843
      4171171117717   4171171177717

25.   24400222433004   24400222433004   25._____
      5300030055000355   5300030055500355
      20000075532002022   20000075532002022

26. 611166640660001116   611166640660001116   26._____
     711130011700110073   711130011700110073
     26666446664476518   26666446664476518

26. 611166640660001116   61116664066001116   26._____
     7111300117001100733   7111300117001100733
     26666446664476518   26666446664476518

Questions 27-30.

DIRECTIONS: Questions 27 through 30 are to be answered by picking the answer which is in the correct numerical order, from the lowest number to the highest number, in each question.

27. A. 44533, 44518, 44516, 44547   27._____
     B. 44516, 44518, 44533, 44547
     C. 44547, 44533, 44518, 44516
     D. 44518, 44516, 44547, 44533

28. A. 95587, 95593, 95601, 95620   28._____
     B. 95601, 95620, 95587, 95593
     C. 95593, 95587, 95601, 95620
     D. 95620, 95601, 95593, 95587

29. A. 232212, 232208, 232232, 232223   29._____
     B. 232208, 232223, 232212, 232232
     C. 232208, 232212, 232223, 232232
     D. 232223, 232232, 232208, 232212

30. A. 113419, 113521, 113462, 113588   30._____
     B. 113588, 113462, 113521, 113419
     C. 113521, 113588, 113419, 113462
     D. 113419, 113462, 113521, 113588

_____

KEY (CORRECT ANSWERS)

1.	C	11.	A	21.	C
2.	B	12.	C	22.	A
3.	D	13.	A	23.	D
4.	A	14.	A	24.	A
5.	C	15.	C	25.	C
6.	B	16.	B	26.	C
7.	D	17.	B	27.	B
8.	A	18.	B	28.	A
9.	D	19.	B	29.	C
10.	C	20.	B	30.	D

_____

CODING
EXAMINATION SECTION
TEST 1

COMMENTARY

An ingenious question-type called coding, involving elements of alphabetizing, filing, name and number comparison, and evaluative judgment and application, has currently won wide acceptance in testing circles for measuring clerical aptitude and general ability, particularly on the senior (middle) grades (levels).

While the directions for this question-type usually vary in detail, the candidate is generally asked to consider groups of names, codes, and numbers, and, then, according to a given plan, to arrange codes in alphabetic order; to arrange these in numerical sequence; to re-arrange columns of names and numbers in correct order; to espy errors in coding; to choose the correct coding arrangement in consonance with the given directions and examples, etc.

This question-type appears to have few parameters in respect to form, substance, or degree of difficulty.

Accordingly, acquaintance with, and practice in the coding question is recommended for the serious candidate.

DIRECTIONS: Column I consists of serial numbers of dollar bills. Column II shows different ways of arranging the corresponding serial numbers.
The serial numbers of dollar bills in Column I begin and end with a capital letter and have an eight-digit number in between. The serial numbers in Column I are to be arranged according to the following rules:

First: In alphabetical order according to the first letter.

Second: When two or more serial numbers have the same first letter, in alphabetical order according to the last letter.

Third: When two or more serial numbers have the same first *and* last letters, in numerical order, beginning with the lowest number

The serial numbers in Column I are numbered (1) through (5) in the order in which they are listed. In Column II the numbers (1) through (5) are arranged in four different ways to show different arrangements of the corresponding serial numbers. Choose the answer in Column II in which the serial numbers are arranged according to the above rules.

Column I		Column II	
1.	E75044127B	A.	4, 1, 3, 2, 5
2.	B96399104A	B.	4, 1, 2, 3, 5
3.	B93939086A	C.	4, 3, 2, 5, 1
4.	B47064465H	D.	3, 2, 5, 4, 1

In the sample question, the four serial numbers starting with B should be put before the serial number starting with E. The serial numbers starting with B and ending with A should be put before the serial number starting with B and ending with H. The three serial numbers starting with B and ending with A should be listed in numerical order, beginning with the lowest number. The correct way to arrange the serial numbers therefore is:

3.	B93939086A	Since the order of arrangement is 3, 2, 5, 4, 1,
2.	B96399104A	the answer to the sample question is D.
5.	B99040922A	
4.	B47064465H	
1.	E75044127B	

	Column I		Column II	

1.
1.	D89143888P	A.	3, 5, 2, 1, 4	1.____
2.	D98143838B	B.	3, 1, 4, 5, 2	
3.	D89113883B	C.	4, 2, 3, 1, 5	
4.	D89148338P	D.	4, 1, 3, 5, 2	
5.	D89148388B			

2.
1.	W62455599E	A.	2, 4, 3, 1, 5	2.____
2.	W62455090F	B.	3, 1, 5, 2, 4	
3.	W62405099E	C.	5, 3, 1, 4, 2	
4.	V62455097F	D.	5, 4, 3, 1, 2	
5.	V62405979E			

3.
1.	N74663826M	A.	2, 4, 5, 3, 1	3.____
2.	M74633286M	B.	2, 5, 4, 1, 3	
3.	N76633228N	C.	1, 2, 5, 3, 4	
4.	M76483686N	D.	2, 5, 1, 4, 3	
5.	M74636688M			

4.
1.	P97560324B	A.	1, 5, 2, 3, 4	4.____
2.	R97663024B	B.	3, 1, 4, 5, 2	
3.	P97503024E	C.	1, 5, 3, 2, 4	
4.	R97563240E	D.	1, 5; 2* 3, 4	
5.	P97652304B			

5.
1.	H92411165G	A.	2, 5, 3, 4, 1	5.____
2.	A92141465G	B.	3, 4, 2, 5, 1	
3.	H92141165C	C.	3, 2, 1, 5, 4	
4.	H92444165C	D.	3, 1, 2, 5, 4	
5.	A92411465G			

6.
1.	X90637799S	A.	4, 3, 5, 2, 1	6.____
2.	N90037696S	B.	5, 4, 2, 1, 3	
3.	Y90677369B	C.	5, 2, 4, 1, 3	
4.	X09677693B	D.	5, 2, 3, 4, 1	
5.	M09673699S			

7.
1.	K78425174L	A.	4, 2, 1, 3, 5	7.____
2.	K78452714C	B.	2, 3, 5, 4, 1	
3.	K78547214N	C.	1, 4, 2, 3, 5	
4.	K78442774C	D.	4, 2, 1, 5, 3	
5.	K78547724M			

8.
1.	P18736652U	A.	1, 3, 4, 5, 2	8.____
2.	P18766352V	B.	1, 5, 2, 3, 4	
3.	T17686532U	C.	3, 4, 5, 1, 2	
4.	T17865523U	D.	5, 2, 1, 3, 4	
5.	P18675332V			

9.
1.	L51138101K	A.	1, 5, 3, 2, 4	9.____
2.	S51138001R	B.	1, 3, 5, 2, 4	
3.	S51188111K	C.	1, 5, 2, 4, 3	
4.	S51183110R	D.	2, 5, 1, 4, 3	
5.	L51188100R			

	Column I		Column II	
10.	1. J28475336D	A.	5, 1, 2, 3, 4	10.____
	2. T28775363D	B.	4, 3, 5, 1, 2	
	3. J27843566P	C.	1, 5, 2, 4, 3	
	4. T27834563P	D.	5, 1, 3, 2, 4	
	5. J28435536D			
11.	1. S55126179E	A.	1, 5, 2, 3, 4	11.____
	2. R55136177Q	B.	3, 4, 1, 5, 2	
	3. P55126177R	C.	3, 5, 2, 1, 4	
	4. S55126178R	D.	4, 3, 1, 5, 2	
	5. R55126180P			
12.	1. T64217813Q	A.	4, 1, 3, 2, 5	12.____
	2. 1642178170	B.	2, 4, 3, 1, 5	
	3. T642178180	C.	4, 1, 5, 2, 3	
	4. I64217811Q	D.	2, 3, 4, 1, 5	
	5. T64217816Q			
13.	1. B33886897B	A.	5, 1, 3, 4, 2	13.____
	2. B38386882B	B.	1, 2, 5, 3, 4	
	3. D33389862B	C.	1, 2, 5, 4, 3	
	4. D33336887D	D.	2, 1, 4, 5, 3	
	5. B38888697D			
14.	1. E11664554M	A.	4, 1, 2, 5, 3	14.____
	2. F11164544M	B.	2, 4, 1, 5, 3	
	3. F11614455N	C.	4, 2, 1, 3, 5	
	4. E11665454M	D.	1, 4, 2, 3, 5	
	5. F16161545N			
15.	1. C86611355W	A.	2, 4, 1, 5, 3	15.____
	2. C68631533V	B.	1, 2, 4, 3, 5	
	3. G88633331W	C.	1, 2, 5, 4, 3	
	4. C68833515V	D.	1, 2, 4, 3, 5	
	5. G68833511W			
16.	1. R73665312J	A.	3, 2, 1, 4, 5	16.____
	2. P73685512J	B.	2, 3, 5, 1, 4	
	3. P73968511J	C.	2, 3, 1, 5, 4	
	4. R73665321K	D.	3, 1, 5, 2, 4	
	5. R63985211K			
17.	1. X33661222U	A.	1, 4, 5, 2, 3	17.____
	2. Y83961323V	B.	4, 5, 1, 3, 2	
	3. Y88991123V	C.	4, 5, 1, 2, 3	
	4. X33691233U	D.	4, 1, 5, 2, 3	
	5. X38691333U			

	Column I		Column II	
18.	1. B22838847W	A.	4, 5, 2, 3, 1	18.____
	2. B28833874V	B.	4, 2, 5, 1, 3	
	3. B22288344X	C.	4, 5, 2, 1, 3	
	4. B28238374V	D.	4, 1, 5, 2, 3	
	5. B28883347V			
19.	1. H44477447G	A.	1, 3, 5, 4, 2	19.____
	2. H47444777G	B.	3, 1, 5, 2, 4	
	3. H74777477C	C.	1, 4, 2, 3, 5	
	4. H44747447G	D.	3, 5, 1, 4, 2	
	5. H77747447C			
20.	1. G11143447G	A.	3, 5, 1, 4, 2	20.____
	2. G15133388C	B.	1, 4, 3, 2, 5	
	3. C15134378G	C.	5, 3, 4, 2, 1	
	4. G11534477C	D.	4, 3, 1, 2, 5	
	5. C15533337C			
21.	1. J96693369F	A.	4, 3, 2, 5, 1	21.____
	2. J66939339F	B.	2, 5, 4, 1, 3	
	3. J96693693E	C.	2, 5, 4, 3, 1	
	4. J96663933E	D.	3, 4, 5, 2, 1	
	5. J69639363F			
22.	1. L15567834Z	A.	3, 1, 5, 2, 4	22.____
	2. P11587638Z	B.	1, 3, 5, 4, 2	
	3. M51567688Z	C.	1, 3, 5, 2, 4	
	4. O55578784Z	D.	3, 1, 5, 4, 2	
	5. N53588783Z			
23.	1. C83261824G	A.	2, 4, 1, 5, 3	23.____
	2. C78361833C	B.	4, 2, 1, 3, 5	
	3. G83261732G	C.	3, 1, 5, 2, 4	
	4. C88261823C	D.	2, 3, 5, 1, 4	
	5. G83261743C			
24.	1. A11710107H	A.	2, 1, 4, 3, 5	24.____
	2. H17110017A	B.	3, 1, 5, 2, 4	
	3. A11170707A	C.	3, 4, 1, 5, 2	
	4. H17170171H	D.	3, 5, 1, 2, 4	
	5. A11710177A			
25.	1. R26794821S	A.	3, 2, 4, 1, 5	25.____
	2. O26794821T	B.	3, 4, 2, 1, 5	
	3. M26794827Z	C.	4, 2, 1, 3, 5	
	4. Q26794821R	D.	5, 4, 1, 2, 3	
	5. S26794821P			

KEY (CORRECT ANSWERS)

1.	A	11.	C
2.	D	12.	B
3.	B	13.	B
4.	C	14.	D
5.	A	15.	A
6.	C	16.	C
7.	D	17.	A
8.	B	18.	B
9.	A	19.	D
10.	D	20.	C

21. A
22. B
23. A
24. D
25. A

———

TEST 2

DIRECTIONS : Questions 1 through 5 consist of a set of letters and numbers located under Column I. For each question, pick the answer (A, B, C, or D) located under Column II which contains *ONLY* letters and numbers that appear in the question in Column 1. *PRINT THE LETTER OF THE CORRECT ANSWER IN THE SPACE AT THE RIGHT.*

SAMPLE QUESTION

Column I	Column II
B-9-P-H-2-Z-N-8-4-M	A. B-4-C-3-R-9
	B. 4-H-P-8-6-N
	C. P-2-Z-8-M-9
	D. 4-B-N-5-E-Z

Choice C is the correct answer because P,2,Z,8,M and 9 all appear in the sample question. All the other choices have at least one letter or number that is not in the question.

	Column I		Column I		
1.	1-7-6-J-L-T-3-S-A-2	A.	J-3-S-A-7-L		1.____
		B.	T-S-A-2-6-5		
		C.	3-7-J-L-S-Z		
		D.	A-7-4-J-L-1		
2.	C-0-Q-5-3-9-H-L-2-7	A.	5-9-T-2-7-Q		2.____
		B.	3-0-6-9-L-C		
		C.	9-L-7-Q-C-3		
		D.	H-Q-4-5-9-7		
3.	P-3-B-C-5-6-0-E-1-T	A.	B-4-6-1-3-T		3.____
		B.	T-B-P-3-E-0		
		C.	5-3-0-E-B-G		
		D.	0-6-P-T-9-B		
4.	U-T-Z-2-4-S-8-6-B-3	A.	2-4-S-V-Z-3		4.____
		B.	B-Z-S-8-3-6		
		C.	4-T-U-8-L-B		
		D.	8-3-T-Z-1-2		
5.	4-D-F-G-C-6-8-3-J-L	A.	T-D-6-8-4-J		5.____
		B.	C-4-3-2-J-F		
		C.	8-3-C-5-G-6		
		D.	C-8-6-J-G-L		

Questions 6 - 12.

DIRECTIONS: Each of the questions numbered 6 through 12 consists of a long series of letters and numbers under Column I and four short series of letters and numbers under Column II. For each question, choose the short series of letters and numbers which is entirely and exactly the same as some part of the long series.

SAMPLE QUESTION:

Column I	Column II
JG13572XY89WB14	A. 1372Y8
	B. XYWB14
	C. 72XY89
	D. J13572

In each of choices A, B, and D, one or more of the letters and numbers in the series in Column I is omitted. Only option C reproduces a segment of the series entirely and exactly. Therefore, C is the CORRECT answer to the sample question.

6. IE227FE383L4700
   A. E27FE3
   B. EF838L
   C. EL4700
   D. 83L470

6._____

7. 77J646G54NPB318
   A. NPB318
   B. J646J5
   C. 4G54NP
   D. C54NPB

7._____

8. 85887T358W24A93
   A. 858887
   B. W24A93
   C. 858W24
   D. 87T353

8._____

9. E104RY796B33H14
   A. 04RY79
   B. E14RYR
   C. 96B3H1
   D. RY7996

9._____

10. W58NP12141DE07M
    A. 8MP121
    B. W58NP1
    C. 14DEO7
    D. 12141D

10._____

11. P473R365M442V5W
    A. P47365
    B. 73P365
    C. 365M44
    D. 5X42V5

11._____

12.   865CG441V21SS59

    A.   1V12SS
    B.   V21SS5
    C.   5GC441
    D.   894CG4

12.____

KEY (CORRECT ANSWERS)

1.	A	7.	A
2.	C	8.	B
3.	B	9.	A
4.	B	10.	D
5.	D	11.	C
6.	D	12.	B

TEST 3

DIRECTIONS : Each question from 1 to 8 consists of a set of letters and numbers. For each question, pick as your answer from the column to the right, the choice which has *ONLY* numbers and letters that are in the question you are answering.

To help you understand what to do, the following sample question is given:

SAMPLE :   B-9-P-H-2-Z-N-8-4-M

    A.   B-4-C-3-E-9
    B.   4-H-P-8-6-N
    C.   P-2-Z-8-M-9
    D.   4-B-N-5-E-2

Choice C is the correct answer because P, 2, Z, 8, M, 9 are in the sample question. All the other choices have at least one letter or number that is not in the question.

Questions 1 through 4 are based on Column I.

Column I

1. X-8-3-I-H-9-4-G-P-U   A. I-G-W-8-2-1   1.____

2. 4-1-2-X-U-B-9-H-7-3   B. U-3-G-9-P-8   2.____

3. U-I-G-2-5-4-W-P-3-B   C. 3-G-I-4-S-U   3.____

4. 3-H-7-G-4-5-I-U-8   D. 9-X-4-7-2-H   4.____

Questions 5 through 8 are based on Column II.

Column II

5. L-2-9-Z-R-8-Q-Y-5-7   A. 8-R-N-3-T-Z   5.____

6. J-L-9-N-Y-8-5-Q-Z-2   B. 2-L-R-5-7-Q   6.____

7. T-Y-3-3-J-Q-2-N-R-Z   C. J-2-8-Z-Y-5   7.____

8. 8-Z-7-T-N-L-1-E-R-3   D. Z-8-9-3-L-5   8.____

KEY (CORRECT ANSWERS)

1.	B	5.	B
2.	D	6.	C
3.	C	7.	A
4.	C	8.	A

———

TEST 4

DIRECTIONS : Questions 1 through 5 have lines of letters and numbers. Each letter should be matched with its number in accordance with the following table:

Letter	F	R	C	A	W	L	E	N	B	T
Matching Number	0	1	2	3	4	5	6	7	8	9

From the table you can determine that the letter F has the matching number 0 below it, the letter R has the matching number 1 below it, etc.

For each question, compare each line of letters and numbers carefully to see if each letter has its correct matching number. If all the letters and numbers are matched correctly in

none of the lines of the question, mark your answer A

only *one* of the lines of the question, mark your answer B

only *two* of the lines of the question, mark your answer C

all three lines of the question, mark your answer D

WBCR	4826
TLBF	9580
ATNE	3986

There is a mistake in the first line because the letter R should have its matching number 1 instead of the number 6. The second line is correct because each letter shown has the correct matching number.

There is a mistake in the third line because the letter N should have the matching number 7 instead of the number 8. Since all the letters and numbers are matched correctly in only one of the lines in the sample, the correct answer is B.

1.		EBCT	6829	1.____
		ATWR	3961	
		NLBW	7584	
2.		RNCT	1729	2.____
		LNCR	5728	
		WAEB	5368	
3.		STWB	7948	3.____
		RABL	1385	
		TAEF	9360	
4.		LWRB	5417	4.____
		RLWN	1647	
		CBWA	2843	
5.		ABTC	3792	
		WCER	5261	
		AWCN	3417	

KEY (CORRECT ANSWERS)

1. C
2. B
3. D
4. B
5. A

TEST 5

DIRECTIONS : Assume that each of the capital letters in the table below represents the name of an employee enrolled in the city employees retirement system. The number directly beneath the letter represents the agency for which the employee works, and the small letter directly beneath represents the code for the employees account.

Name of Employee	L	O	T	Q	A	M	R	N	C
Agency	3	4	5	9	8	7	2	1	6
Account Code	r	f	b	i	d	t	g	e	n

In each of the following Questions 1 through 10, the agency code numbers and the account code letters in Columns 2 and 3 should correspond to the capital letters in Column 1 and should be in the same consecutive order. For each question, look at each column carefully and mark your answer as follows:

If there are one or more errors in *Column 2 only,* mark your answer *A,*

If there are one or more errors in *Column 3 only,* mark your answer B.

If there are one or more errors in Column 2 *and* one or more errors in Column 3, mark your answer C.

If there are *NO* errors in either column, mark your answer D,

The following sample question is given to help you understand the procedure.

Column 1	Column 2	Column 3
T Q L M O C	5 8 3 7 4 6	b i r t f n

In Column 2, the second agency code number (corresponding to letter Q) should be "9", not "8". Column 3 is coded correctly to Column 1. Since there is an error only in Column 2, the correct answer is A.

	Column 1	Column 2	Column 3	
1.	Q L N R C A	9 3 1 2 6 8	i f e g n d	1.____
2.	N R M O T C	1 2 7 5 4 6	e g f t b n	2.____
3.	R C T A L M	2 6 5 8 3 7	g n d b r t	3.____
4.	T A M L O N	5 7 8 3 4 1	b d t r f e	4.____
5.	A N T O R M	8 1 5 4 2 7	d e b i g t	5.____
6.	M R A L O N	7 2 8 3 4 1	t g d r f e	6.____
7.	C T N Q R O	6 5 7 9 2 4	n d e i g f	7.____
8.	Q M R O T A	9 7 2 4 5 8	i t g f b d	8.____
9.	R Q M C O L	2 9 7 4 6 3	g i t n f r	9.____
10.	N O M R T Q	1 4 7 2 5 9	e f t g b i	10.____

KEY (CORRECT ANSWERS)

1.	D	6.	D
2.	C	7.	C
3.	B	8.	D
4.	A	9.	A
5.	B	10.	D

―――――

TEST 6

DIRECTIONS: Each of Questions 1 through 6 consists of three lines of code letters and numbers. The numbers on each line should correspond to the code letters on the same line in accordance with the table below.

Code Letter	D	Y	K	L	P	U	S	R	A	E
Corresponding Number	0	1	2	3	4	5	6	7	8	9

On some of the lines an error exists in the coding. Compare the letters and numbers in each question carefully. If you find an error or errors on

only *one* of the lines in the question, mark your answer A;

any *two* lines in the question, mark your answer B;

all *three* lines in the question, mark your answer C;

none of the lines in the question, mark your answer D.

SAMPLE QUESTION
KSRYELD	-	2671930
SAPUEKL	-	6845913
RYKADLP	-	5128034

In the above sample, the first line is correct since each code letter listed has the correct corresponding number. On the second line, an error exists because code letter K should have number 2 instead of number 1. On the third line, an error exists because the code letter R should have the number 7 instead of the number 5. Since there are errors on two of the three lines, the correct answer is B.

Now answer the following questions, using the same procedure.

1. YPUSRLD   -   1456730   1._____
   UPSAEDY   -   5648901
   PREYDKS   -   4791026

2. AERLPUS   -   8973456   2._____
   DKLYDPA   -   0231048
   UKLDREP   -   5230794

3. DAPUSLA   -   0845683   3._____
   YKLDLPS   -   1230356
   PUSKYDE   -   4562101

4. LRPUPDL   -   3745403   4._____
   SUPLEDR   -   6543907
   PKEYDLU   -   4291025

5. KEYDESR   -   2910967   5._____
   PRSALEY   -   4678391
   LSRAYSK   -   3687162

6. YESREYL   -   1967913   6._____
   PLPRAKY   -   4346821
   YLPSRDU   -   1346705

KEY (CORRECT ANSWERS)

1. A
2. D
3. C
4. A
5. B
6. A

———

NAME AND NUMBER CHECKING

EXAMINATION SECTION
TEST 1

DIRECTIONS: Each question consists of a name, address, and social security number, arranged in 2 lists. List I is correct, but some mistakes were made in copying the information to List II. For each question, you must check to see if there are any mistakes in List II. Mark your answer A if there are no mistakes in List II. Mark your answer B if there is a mistake in List II.

LIST I	LIST II	
1. CAROLE ANN DONAHUE 47 MANN TERRACE 074-42-0911	Carole Ann Donahue 47 Mann Terrace 074-42-0911	1._____
2. JOHN PETERSON 1411-26TH STREET 472-09-4442	John Peterson 1411-26th Street 472-09-4443	2._____
3. PAULINE JACOBSON 76 COOLIDGE AVENUE 034-47-1182	Pauline Jacobson 76 Coolige Avenue 034-47-1182	3._____
4. JANET SILLS 320 WEST 86TH STREET 474-09-2211	Janet Sils 320 West 86th Street 474-09-2211	4._____
5. ABELARD SIMS 47 ST. MARK'S PLACE 842-57-8738	Abelard Sims 47 St. Mark's Place 842-57-8738	5._____
6. ROGER STURTYVENT 87 ELLIS AVENUE 298-46-8853	Roger Sturytvent 87 Ellis Avenue 298-46-8853	6._____
7. ALICIA BARNETT 42 WORTH STREET 047-42-0091	Alicia Barnett 42 Worth Street 042-47-0091	7._____
8. BARRY KNOWLES 283 WEST 43RD STREET 681-42-5712	Barry Knowles 283 West 43rd Street 681-42-5712	8._____
9. ELIZABETH HOWE 16 ELM STREET 442-01-0011	Elizabeth Howes 16 Elm Street 442-01-0011	9._____
10. BRUCE DOYLE 14 MAIN STREET 141-01-4411	Bruce Doyle 14 Main Street 144-01-4411	10._____

LIST I	LIST II	
11. MICHAEL O'BRIAN 42 CHELSEA COURT 191-11-8776	Michael O'Brien 42 Chelsea Court 191-11-8776	11.____
12. CHARLES DOWD 2 PETERSON PLACE 862-75-6996	Charles Dowd 2 Peterson Place 862-75-6996	12.____
13. JUDITH KAPLAN 1876 SO. 4TH STREET 151-49-7889	Judith Kaplan 1876 So. 4th Street 151-94-7889	13.____
14. MARIA PUCCINI 98 PINE STREET 089-47-0211	Maria Pucini 98 Pine Street 089-47-0211	14.____
15. GABRIELLE GIATINO 11 WEST 96TH STREET 477-98-1186	Gabrielle Giatino 11 West 69th Street 477-98-1186	15.____
16. SUZANNE PATTERSON 82 BROOKLYN BLVD. 897-42-0966	Suzanne Patterson 82 Brooklyn Blvd. 897-42-0966	16.____
17. ANNA PANERO 8 WIDMONT PLACE 477-89-4211	Anna Panero 8 Widmont Place 474-89-4211	17.____
18. WILLIAM BUTLER 19 BRIDGE STREET 118-09-4776	William Butler 19 Bridge Street 118-09-4776	18.____
19. EMILE KNUDSON 78 CONCORD STREET 877-00-0011	Emiel Knudson 78 Concord Street 877-00-0011	19.____
20. MILKA FLORES 1811 31ST STREET 865-51-9962	Milka Flores 1181 31st Street 865-51-9962	20.____
21. MARIANNE CONKLIN 87 SO. MAPLE STREET 742-98-0781	Marianne Conklin 87 So. Maple Street 742-89-0781	21.____
22. DONALD MARIN 47 KIRSTEN STREET 870-91-4173	Donald Marin 47 Kirstein Street 870-91-4173	22.____
23. KLAUS GUDOFF 11 CATHERINE AVENUE 811-46-1950	Klause Gudoff 11 Catherine Avenue 811-46-1950	23.____

LIST I	LIST II	
24. PAUL GOODMAN 111 BRIDGE ROAD 470-91-8771	Paul Goodman 171 Bridge Road 470-91-8771	24.____
25. BLYTHE SARGENT 9 GASTON PLACE 247-83-5471	Blythe Sargent 9 Gaston Place 247-83-5471	25.____

KEY (CORRECT ANSWERS)

ERROR IN LIST II

1.	A	
2.	B	472-09-444<u>3</u>
3.	B	76 Cool<u>i</u>ge Avenue
4.	B	Si<u>ls</u>
5.	A	
6.	B	Stur<u>y</u>tvent
7.	B	04<u>2</u>-4<u>7</u>-0091
8.	A	
9.	B	Howe<u>s</u>
10.	B	14<u>4</u>-01-4411
11.	B	O'Bri<u>e</u>n
12.	A	
13.	B	151-<u>94</u>-7889
14.	B	Pu<u>c</u>ini
15.	B	11 West <u>69</u>th Street
16.	A	
17.	B	47<u>4</u>-89-4211
18.	A	
19.	B	Emi<u>el</u>
20.	B	1<u>18</u>1 31st Street
21.	B	742-<u>89</u>-0781
22.	B	47 Kirste<u>i</u>n Street
23.	B	Klaus<u>e</u>
24.	B	1<u>7</u>1 Bridge Road
25.	A	

125

TEST 2

DIRECTIONS: Each question consists of a name, address, and social security number, arranged in 2 lists. List I is correct, but some mistakes were made in copying the information to List II. For each question, you must check to see if there are any mistakes in List II. Mark your answer A if there are no mistakes in List II. Mark your answer B if there is a mistake in List II.

LIST I	LIST II	
1. MARK ROSS 18 BRADLEY STREET 671-91-0710	Mark Ross 18 Bradley Street 671-91-0170	1.____
2. SELMA BLACK 687 AVENUE B 971-68-5441	Selma Black 687 Avenue B 971-68-5441	2.____
3. ADA BLUESTEIN 14 PARK PLACE 777-06-9944	Ada Blustein 14 Park Place 777-06-9944	3.____
4. MELVIN KUPERSTEIN 14 NATIONAL BLVD. 687-91-0422	Melwin Kuperstein 14 National Blvd. 687-91-0422	4.____
5. LIONEL ROGERS 78 AMSTERDAM AVENUE 242-89-7899	Lionel Rogers 78 Amsterdam Avenue 242-89-7989	5.____
6. HOWARD MICHAELS 7 LYDIA PLACE 891-01-8711	Howard Michael 7 Lydia Place 891-01-8711	6.____
7. CHARLES WEISSMANN 1862 YORK AVENUE 289-47-2298	Charles Weismann 1862 York Avenue 289-47-2298	7.____
8. SYLVESTER GREENE 11 AUDIO ROAD 781-24-5577	Sylvester Greene 11 Audio Road 781-24-5577	8.____
9. MICHELLE LAMANS 82 POLO DRIVE 161-02-4278	Michelle LaMans 82 Polo Drive 161-02-4278	9.____
10. ROBERTA FARNES 1682 NIPPON STREET 191-24-7811	Robert Farnes 1682 Nippon Street 191-24-7811	10.____

LIST I	LIST II	
11. ELLIOT GOODMAN 78 ELF DRIVE 427-98-5671	Elliot Goodman 78 Elf Drive 427-98-5761	11.____
12. THOMAS BENSON 87 YACHT ROAD 988-07-4733	Thomas Benson 87 Yacht Road 988-07-4733	12.____
13. SHARON IRVING 22 CLIFFSIDE DRIVE 486-86-8811	Sharon Irving 22 Cliffside Drive 486-68-8811	13.____
14. ADAM TOWER 211 EAST 116TH STREET 142-17-8799	Adam Tower 211 East 16th Street 142-17-8799	14.____
15. DARLEEN MONTGOMERY 1487 BROADWAY 866-20-0791	Darleen Montgomery 1487 Broadway 866-02-0791	15.____
16. H. DOUGLAS KELLY 111-20 AVENUE M 168-29-4757	H. Douglas Kelly 111-20 Avenue N 168-29-4757	16.____
17. DANIEL MCDONALD 18 EIGHT-MILE DRIVE 299-07-4856	Daniel McDonald 18 Eight-Mile Drive 299-07-4856	17.____
18. GEORGE WOLFF 19 WESTERLY PLACE 555-01-4782	George Wolff 19 Westerly Place 555-01-4782	18.____
19. BURTON DONOVAN 1473 OCEAN PARKWAY 247-54-0667	Burton Donavon 1473 Ocean Parkway 247-54-0667	19.____
20. JULIAN SCHLOSS 87 MOUNTAIN ROAD 287-81-1248	Julian Schloss 87 Mountain Road 287-81-1248	20.____
21. PAMELA AUSTIN 3342 92ND STREET 373-02-4791	Pamela Austin 3342 42nd Street 373-02-4791	21.____
22. DAVID BALINI 43 PECK AVENUE 297-87-1142	David Balnini 43 Peck Avenue 297-87-1142	22.____
23. DORIAN FOX 601 COLUMBUS AVENUE 988-37-2799	Dorian Fox 601 Columbus Avenue 988-37-2779	23.____

LIST I	LIST II	
24. EVELYN COOKE 98 ALBANIA DRIVE 422-27-8783	Evelyne Cooke 98 Albania Drive 422-27-8783	24.____
25. RICHARD PERLOW 7 SO. MAPLE STREET 422-09-7111	Richard Perlow 7 So. Maple Street 422-09-7111	25.____

KEY (CORRECT ANSWERS)

ERROR IN LIST II

1.	B	671-91-0170
2.	A	
3.	B	Blustein
4.	B	Melwin
5.	B	242-89-7989
6.	B	Michael_
7.	B	Weismann
8.	A	
9.	A	
10.	B	Robert_
11.	B	427-98-5761
12.	A	
13.	B	486-68-8811
14.	B	211 East 16th Street
15.	B	866-02-0791
16.	B	111-20 Ave. N
17.	A	
18.	A	
19.	B	Donavon
20.	A	
21.	B	3342 42nd Street
22.	B	Balnini
23.	B	988-37-2779
24.	B	Evelyne
25.	A	

TEST 3

DIRECTIONS: Each question consists of a name, address, and social security number, arranged in 2 lists. List I is correct, but some mistakes were made in copying the information to List II. For each question, you must check to see if there are any mistakes in List II. Mark your answer A if there are no mistakes in List II. Mark your answer B if there is a mistake in List II.

LIST I	LIST II	
1. STANLEY KORASH 14 MIDDLE STREET 271-76-7663	Stanly Korash 14 Middle Street 271-76-7663	1.____
2. MILDRED BACH 5 GOLDEN COURT 866-01-7115	Mildred Bach 5 Golden Court 856-01-7115	2.____
3. RAJIV RUSHDIE 330 EAST 10TH STREET 472-81-9144	Rajiv Rushdie 330 East 10th Street 472-81-9114	3.____
4. LEAN CHOV 63 MOTT STREET 249-01-0677	Lean Chov 63 Mott Street 249-01-0677	4.____
5. NELLE SHAW 783 WARREN AVENUE 861-21-2115	Neile Shaw 783 Warren Avenue 861-21-2115	5.____
6. PHILIP LEE 6 TANDY COURT 297-86-1142	Philip Lee 6 Tandy Court 297-68-1142	6.____
7. ARMANDO SAVAS 663 CAMINO REAL 211-07-8776	Armando Savas 663 Camino Rael 211-07-8776	7.____
8. KENNETH BELLOWS 71 PINE STREET 877-11-0119	Kenneth Bellows 17 Pine Street 877-11-0119	8.____
9. ROSE GOLDMAN 16 ELIZABETH STREET 247-91-4855	Rose Goldman 16 Elizabeth Street 247-91-4855	9.____
10. KYLIE ANDREWS 51 TIMBERLANE ROAD 687-54-0345	Kylie Andrews 51 Timbreland Road 687-54-0345	10.____

LIST I

11. ANNAMARIE PINKERTON
16 WINSLOW LANE
879-23-2711

12. GERTRUDE GREY
47 CORTLAND AVENUE
470-01-2291

13. PRISCILLA TUNNIE
18 JACKARD LANE
421-27-0733

14. ALICE ALLEN
29 WEST 476TH STREET
279-09-4291

15. CARTER BONNARD
311 EAST 86TH STREET
428-08-8773

16. PETER BISHOP
79-09 S.W. 11TH STREET
853-53-7711

17. ALAN PURCELL
2 MIDDLE COURT
454-29-0733

18. OBDAYA GREENE
154 WEST 107TH STREET
237-21-0734

19. ELYSSA TARENBAUM
42 WEST 9TH STREET
731-07-6622

20. HENRY ROBBINS
811 CORTLAND AVENUE
279-34-0011

21. HELEN SAUNDERS
91 GREEN TERRACE ROAD
681-29-4731

22. NAT FOREMAN
87 MASTERS AVENUE
879-24-0731

LIST II

Annamarie Pinkerton
16 Winslow Lane
879-23-2711   11.____

Gertrude Gray
47 Cortland Avenue
470-01-2291   12.____

Priscilla Tunnie
18 Jackard Lane
421-27-0773   13.____

Alice Allen
29 West 476th Street
279-09-4291   14.____

Carter Bonnard
311 East 86th Street
488-08-8773   15.____

Peter Bishop
79-09 S.W. 11th Street
853-53-7711   16.____

Allen Purcell
2 Middle Court
454-29-0733   17.____

Obdaya Green
154 West 107th Street
237-21-0734   18.____

Elyssa Tarenbaum
42 West 9th Street
731-07-6622   19.____

Henry Robbins
811 Cortlande Avenue
279-34-0011   20.____

Helen Saunders
91 Green Terrace Road
681-29-4771   21.____

Nat Forman
87 Masters Avenue
879-24-0731   22.____

LIST I	LIST II	
23. ELIZABETH CARDINALI 41 MIRA LANE 787-29-3411	Elizabeth Cardinali 41 Mira Lane 787-29-3411	23.____
24. FRANK SMYTHE 56 FRANKLIN BLVD. 298-78-8711	Frank Smythe 56 Franklin Blvd. 299-78-8711	24.____
25. ANTONIO FIORELLO 111 WEST 90TH STREET 249-87-1106	Antonio Fiorello 111 West 90th Street 249-87-1106	25.____

KEY (CORRECT ANSWERS)

ERROR IN LIST II

1.	B	Stanly
2.	B	856-01-7115
3.	B	472-81-9114
4.	A	
5.	B	Neile
6.	B	297-68-1142
7.	B	663 Camino Rael
8.	B	17 Pine Street
9.	A	
10.	B	51 Timbrelane Road
11.	A	
12.	B	Gray
13.	B	421-27-0773
14.	A	
15.	B	488-08-8773
16.	A	
17.	B	Allen
18.	B	Green_
19.	A	
20.	B	Cortlande Avenue
21.	B	681-29-4771
22.	B	Forman
23.	A	
24.	B	299-78-8711
25.	A	

FILING

EXAMINATION SECTION
TEST 1

DIRECTIONS: Questions 1 through 8 each show in Column I names written on four cards (lettered w, x, y, z) which have to be filed. You are to choose the option (lettered A, B, C, or D) in Column II which *BEST* represents the proper order of filing according to the Rules for Alphabetic Filing, given before, and the sample question given below. Print the letter of the correct answer in the space at the right.

SAMPLE QUESTION

Column I	Column II
w. Jane Earl	A. w, y, z, x
x. James A. Earle	B. y, w, z, x
y. James Earl	C. x, y, w, z
z. J. Earle	D. x, w, y, z

The correct way to file the cards is:
   y.   James Earl
   w.   Jane Earl
   z.   J. Earle
   x.   James A. Earle

The correct filing order is shown by the letters, y, w, z, x (in that sequence). Since, in Column II, B appears in front of the letters, y, w, z, x (in that sequence), B is the correct answer to the sample question.

Now answer the following questions using that same procedure.

Column I | Column II |
--- | --- | ---
1. w. James Rothschild
x. Julius B. Rothchild
y. B. Rothstein
z. Brian Joel Rothenstein | A. x, z, w, y
B. x, w, z, y
C. z, y, w, x
D. z, w, x, y | 1._____
2. w. George S. Wise
x. S. G. Wise
y. Geo. Stuart Wise
z. Prof. Diana Wise | A. w, y, z, x
B. x, w, y, z
C. y, x, w, z
D. z, w, y, x | 2._____
3. w. 10th Street Bus Terminal
x. Buckingham Travel Agency
y. The Buckingham Theater
z. Burt Tompkins Studio | A. x, z, w, y
B. y, x, w, z
C. w, z, y, x
D. x, w, y, z | 3._____
4. w. National Council of American
           Importers
x. National Chain Co. of Providence
y. National Council on Alcoholism
z. National Chain Co. | A. w, y, x, z
B. x, z, w, y
C. z, x, w, y
D. z, x, y, w | 4._____

5.	w.	Dr. Herbert Alvary	A.	w, y, x, z	5.____
	x.	Mr. Victor Alvarado	B.	z, w, x, y	
	y.	Alvar Industries	C.	y, z, x, w	
	z.	V. Alvarado	D.	w, z, x, y	

6.	w.	Joan MacBride	A.	w, x, z, y	6.____
	x.	Wm. Mackey	B.	w, y, z, x	
	y.	Roslyn McKenzie	C.	w, z, x, y	
	z.	Winifred Mackey	D.	w, y, x, z	

7.	w.	3 Way Trucking Co.	A.	y, x, z, w	7.____
	x.	3rd Street Bakery	B.	y, z, w, x	
	y.	380 Realty Corp.	C.	x, y, z, w	
	z.	Three Lions Pub	D.	x, y, w, z	

8.	w.	Miss Rose Leonard	A.	z, w, x, y	8.____
	x.	Rev. Leonard Lucas	B.	w, z, y, x	
	y.	Sylvia Leonard Linen Shop	C.	w, x, z, y	
	z.	Rose S. Leonard	D.	z, w, y, x	

_____

KEY (CORRECT ANSWERS)

1. A
2. D
3. B
4. D
5. C
6. A
7. C
8. B

_____

TEST 2

DIRECTIONS: Questions 1 through 7 each show in Column I four names (lettered w, x, y, z) which have to be entered in an agency telephone directory. You are to choose the option (lettered A, B, C, or D) in Column II which *BEST* represents the proper order for entering them according to the Rules for Alphabetic Filing, given before, and the sample question given below.

SAMPLE QUESTION

Column I		Column II	
w.	Doris Jenkin	A.	w, y, z, x
x.	Donald F. Jenkins	B.	y, w, z, x
y.	Donald Jenkin	C.	x, y, w, z
z.	D. Jenkins	D.	x, w, y, z

The correct way to enter these names is:

y. Donald Jenkin
w. Doris Jenkin
z. D. Jenkins
x. Donald F. Jenkins

The correct order is shown by the letters y, w, z, x, in that sequence. Since, in Column II, B appears in front of the letters y, w, z, x, in that sequence, B is the correct answer to the sample question.

Now answer the following questions using the same procedure.

		Column I		Column II	
1.	w.	Lawrence Robertson	A.	x, y, w, z	1.____
	x.	Jack L. Robinson	B.	w, z, x, y	
	y.	John Robinson	C.	z, w, x, y	
	z.	William B. Roberson	D.	z, w, y, x	
2.	w.	P. N. Figueredo	A.	y, x, z, w	2.____
	x.	M. Alice Figueroa	B.	x, z, w, y	
	y.	Jose Figueredo	C.	x, w, z, y	
	z.	M. Alicia Figueroa	D.	y, w, x, z	
3.	w.	George Steven Keats	A.	y, x, w, z	3.____
	x.	George S. Keats	B.	z, y, x, w	
	y.	G. Samuel Keats	C.	x, z, w, y	
	z.	Dr. Samuel Keats	D.	w, z, x, y	
4.	w.	V. Merchant	A.	w, x, y, z	4.____
	x.	Dr. William Mercher	B.	w, y, z, x	
	y.	Prof. Victor Merchant	C.	z, y, w, x	
	z.	Dr. Walter Merchan	D.	z, w, y, x	
5.	w.	Brian McCoy	A.	z, x, y, w	5.____
	x.	William Coyne	B.	y, w, z, x	
	y.	Mr. William MacCoyle	C.	x, z, y, w	
	z.	Dr. D. V. Coyne	D.	w, y, z, x	

6.
   w. Ms. M. Rosie Buchanan
   x. Rosalyn M. Buchanan
   y. Rosie Maria Buchanan
   z. Rosa Marie Buchanan

   A. z, y, x, w
   B. w, z, x, y
   C. w, z, y, x
   D. z, x, y, w

   6.____

7.
   w. Prof. Jonathan Praga
   x. Dr. Joan Prager
   y. Alan VanPrague
   z. Alexander Prague

   A. w, z, y, x
   B. w, x, z, y
   C. x, w, z, y
   D. x, w, y, z

   7.____

KEY (CORRECT ANSWERS)

1. C
2. D
3. A
4. D
5. A
6. B
7. B

TEST 3

DIRECTIONS: Questions 1 through 10 each show in Column I names written on four cards (lettered w, x, y, z) which have to be filed. You are to choose the option (lettered A, B, C, or D) in Column II which *BEST* represents the proper order of filing according to the rules and sample question given below. The cards are to be filed according to the Rules for Alphabetical Filing, given before, and the sample question given below.

SAMPLE QUESTION

Column I		Column II	
w.	Jane Earl	A.	w, y, z, x
x.	James A. Earle	B.	y, w, z, x
y.	James Earl	C.	x, y, w, z
z.	J. Earle	D.	x, w, y, z

The correct way to file the cards is:

y.	James Earl
w.	Jane Earl
z.	J. Earle
x.	James A. Earle

The correct filing order is shown by the letters y, w, z, x (in that order). Since, in Column II, B appears in front of the letters y, w, z, x (in that order), B is the correct answer to the sample question.

Now answer Questions 1 through 10 using the same procedure.

	Column I		Column II		
1.	w. John Smith	A.	w, x, y, z		1.____
	x. Joan Smythe	B.	y, z, x, w		
	y. Gerald Schmidt	C.	y, z, w, x		
	z. Gary Schmitt	D.	z, y, w, x		
2.	w. A. Black	A.	w, x, y, z		2.____
	x. Alan S. Black	B.	w, y, x, z		
	y. Allan Black	C.	w, y, z, x		
	z. Allen A. Black	D.	x, w, y, z		
3.	w. Samuel Haynes	A.	w, x, y, z		3.____
	x. Sam C. Haynes	B.	x, w, z, y		
	y. David Haynes	C.	y, z, w, x		
	z. Dave L. Haynes	D.	z, y, x, w		
4.	w. Lisa B. McNeil	A.	x, y, w, z		4.____
	x. Tom MacNeal	B.	x, z, y, w		
	y. Lisa McNeil	C.	y, w, z, x		
	z. Lorainne McNeal	D.	z, x, y, w		
5.	w. Larry Richardson	A.	w, y, x, z		5.____
	x. Leroy Richards	B.	y, x, z, w		
	y. Larry S. Richards	C.	y, z, x, w		
	z. Leroy C. Richards	D.	x, w, z, y		

6.
   w. Arlene Lane
   x. Arlene Cora Lane
   y. Arlene Clair Lane
   z. Arlene C. Lane

   A. w, z, y, x
   B. w, z, x, y
   C. y, x, z, w
   D. z, y, w, x

6.____

7.
   w. Betty Fish
   x. Prof. Ann Fish
   y. Norma Fisch
   z. Dr. Richard Fisch

   A. w, x, z, y
   B. x, w, y, z
   C. y, z, x, w
   D. z, y, w, x

7.____

8.
   w. Dr. Anthony David Lukak
   x. Mr. Steven Charles Lucas
   y. Mr. Anthony J. Lukak
   z. Prof. Steven C. Lucas

   A. w, y, z, x
   B. x, z, w, y
   C. z, x, y, w
   D. z, x, w, y

8.____

9.
   w. Martha Y. Lind
   x. Mary Beth Linden
   y. Martha W. Lind
   z. Mary Bertha Linden

   A. w, y, z, x
   B. w, y, x, z
   C. y, w, z, x
   D. y, w, x, z

9.____

10.
   w. Prof. Harry Michael MacPhelps
   x. Mr. Horace M. MacPherson
   y. Mr. Harold M. McPhelps
   z. Prof. Henry Martin MacPherson

   A. w, z, x, y
   B. w, y, z, x
   C. z, x, w, y
   D. x, z, y, w

10.____

KEY (CORRECT ANSWERS)

1.	C	6.	A
2.	A	7.	C
3.	D	8.	D
4.	B	9.	C
5.	B	10.	A

TEST 4

DIRECTIONS: Answer Questions 1 through 5 on the basis of the following information:

A certain shop keeps an informational card file on all suppliers and merchandise. On each card is the supplier's name, the contract number for the merchandise he supplies, and a delivery date for the merchandise. In this filing system, the supplier's name is filed alphabetically, the contract number for the merchandise is filed numerically, and the delivery date is filed chronologically.

In Questions 1 through 5 there are five notations numbered 1 through 5 shown in Column I. Each notation is made up of a supplier's name, a contract number, and a date which is to be filed according to the following rules:

First: File in alphabetical order;
Second: When two or more notations have the same supplier, file according to the contract number in numerical order beginning with the lowest number;
Third: When two or more notations have the same supplier and contract number, file according to the date beginning with the earliest date.

In Column II the numbers 1 through 5 are arranged in four ways to show four different orders in which the merchandise information might
be filed. Pick the answer (A., B, C, or D) in Column II in which the notations are arranged according to the above filing rules.

SAMPLE QUESTION

	Column I			Column II
1.	Cluney (4865) 6/17/02		A.	2, 3, 4, 1, 5
2.	Roster (2466) 5/10/01		B.	2, 5, 1, 3, 4
3.	Altool (7114) 10/15/02		C.	3, 2, 1, 4, 5
4.	Cluney (5296) 12/18/01		D.	3, 5, 1, 4, 2
5.	Cluney (4865) 4/8/02			

The correct way to file the cards is:

3.	Altool	(7114) 10/15/02
5.	Cluney	(4865) 4/8/02
1.	Cluney	(4865) 6/17/02
4.	Cluney	(5276) 12/18/01
2.	Roster	(2466) 5/10/01

Since the correct filing order is 3, 5, 1, 4, 2, the answer to the sample question is D. Now answer Questions 1 through 5.

		Column I				Column II	
1.	1.	warren	(96063)	3/30/03	A.	2, 4, 3, 5, 1	1.____
	2.	moore	(21237)	9/4/04	B.	2, 3, 5, 4, 1	
	3.	newman	(10050)	12/12/03	C.	4, 5, 2, 3, 1	
	4.	downs	(81251)	1/2/03	D.	4, 2, 3, 5, 1	
	5.	oliver	(60145)	6/30/04			

2.
1. Henry (40552) 7/6/04
2. Boyd (91251) 9/1/03
3. George (8196) 12/12/03
4. George (31096) 1/12/04
5. West (6109) 8/9/03

A. 5, 4, 3, 1, 2
B. 2, 3, 4, 1, 5
C. 2, 4, 3, 1, 5
D. 5, 2, 3, 1, 4

2.____

3.
1. Salba (4670) 9/7/03
2. Salba (51219) 3/1/03
3. Crete (81562) 7/1/04
4. Salba (51219) 1/11/04
5. Texi (31549) 1/25/03

A. 5, 3, 1, 2, 4
B. 3, 1, 2, 4, 5
C. 3, 5, 4, 2, 1
D. 5, 3, 4, 2, 1

3.____

4.
1. Crayone (87105) 6/10/04
2. Shamba (49210) 1/5/03
3. Valiant (3152) 5/1/04
4. Valiant (3152) 1/9/04
5. Poro (59613) 7/1/03

A. 1, 2, 5, 3, 4
B. 1, 5, 2, 3, 4
C. 1, 5, 3, 4, 2
D. 1, 5, 2, 4, 3

4.____

5.
1. Mackie (42169) 12/20/03
2. Lebo (5198) 9/12/02
3. Drummon (99631) 9/9/04
4. Lebo (15311) 1/25/02
5. Harvin (81765) 6/2/03

A. 3, 2, 1, 5, 4
B. 3, 2, 4, 5, 1
C. 3, 5, 2, 4, 1
D. 3, 5, 4, 2, 1

5.____

KEY (CORRECT ANSWERS)

1. D
2. B
3. B
4. D
5. C

TEST 5

DIRECTIONS: Each of Questions 1 through 8 represents five cards to be filed, numbered 1 through 5 in Column I. Each card is made up of the employee's name, the date of a work assignment, and the work assignment code number shown in parentheses. The cards are to be filed according to the following rules:

First: File in alphabetical order;
Second: When two or more cards have the same employee's name, file according to the assignment date beginning with the earliest date;
Third: When two or more cards have the same employee's name and the same date, file according to the work assignment number beginning with the lowest number.

Column II shows the cards arranged in four different orders. Pick the answer (A, B, C, or D) in Column II which shows the cards arranged correctly according to the above filing rules.

SAMPLE QUESTION

	Column I				Column II
1.	Cluney	4/8/02	(486503)	A.	2, 3, 4, 1, 5
2.	Roster	5/10/01	(246611)	B.	2, 5, 1, 3, 4
3.	Altool	10/15/02	(711433)	C.	3, 2, 1, 4, 5
4.	Cluney	12/18/02	(527610)	D.	3, 5, 1, 4, 2
5.	Cluney	4/8/02	(486500)		

The correct way to file the cards is:
3. Altool 10/15/02 (711433)
5. Cluney 4/8/02 (486500)
1. Cluney 4/8/02 (486503)
4. Cluney 12/18/02 (527610)
2. Roster 5/10/01 (246611)

The correct filing order is shown by the numbers in front of each name (3, 5, 1, 4, 2). The answer to the sample question is the letter in Column II in front of the numbers 3, 5, 1, 4, 2. This answer is D.

Now answer Questions 1 through 8 according to these rules.

1.						Column II	1._____
	1.	Kohls	4/2/02	(125677)	A.	1, 2, 3, 4, 5	
	2.	Keller	3/21/02	(129698)	B.	3, 2, 1, 4, 5	
	3.	Jackson	4/10/02	(213541)	C.	3, 1, 2, 4, 5	
	4.	Richards	1/9/03	(347236)	D.	5, 2, 1, 3, 4	
	5.	Richmond	12/11/01	(379321)			

2.							2._____
	1.	Burroughs	5/27/02	(237896)	A.	1, 4, 3, 2, 5	
	2.	Charlson	1/16/02	(114537)	B.	4, 1, 5, 3, 2	
	3.	Carlsen	12/2/02	(114377)	C.	1, 4, 3, 5, 2	
	4.	Burton	5/1/02	(227096)	D.	4, 1, 3, 5, 2	
	5.	Charlson	12/2/02	(114357)			

3.	A.	Ungerer	11/11/02	(537924)		A.	1, 5, 3, 2, 4		3.__
	B.	Winters	1/10/02	(657834)		B.	5, 1, 3, 4, 2		
	C.	Ventura	12/1/02	(698694)		C.	3, 5, 1, 2, 4		
	D.	Winters	10/11/02	(675654)		D.	1, 5, 3, 4, 2		
	E.	Ungaro	1/10/02	(684325)					
4.	1.	Norton	3/12/03	(071605)		A.	1, 4, 2, 3, 5		4.__
	2.	Morris	2/26/03	(068931)		B.	3, 5, 2, 4, 1		
	3.	Morse	5/12/03	(142358)		C.	2, 4, 3, 5, 1		
	4.	Morris	2/26/03	(068391)		D.	4, 2, 5, 3, 1		
	5.	Morse	2/26/03	(068391)					
5.	1.	Eger	4/19/02	(874129)		A.	3, 4, 1, 2, 5		5.__
	2.	Eihler	5/19/03	(875329)		B.	1, 4, 5, 2, 3		
	3.	Ehrlich	11/19/02	(874839)		C.	4, 1, 3, 2, 5		
	4.	Eger	4/19/02	(876129)		D.	1, 4, 3, 5, 2		
	5.	Eihler	5/19/02	(874239)					
6.	1.	Johnson	12/21/02	(786814)		A.	2, 4, 3, 5, 1		6.__
	2.	Johns	12/21/03	(801024)		B.	4, 2, 5, 3, 1		
	3.	Johnson	12/12/03	(762814)		C.	4, 5, 3, 1, 2		
	4.	Jackson	12/12/03	(862934)		D.	5, 3, 1, 2, 4		
	5.	Johnson	12/12/03	(762184)					
7.	1.	Fuller	7/12/02	(598310)		A.	2, 1, 5, 4, 3		7.__
	2.	Fuller	7/2/02	(598301)		B.	1, 2, 4, 5, 3		
	3.	Fuller	7/22/02	(598410)		C.	1, 4, 5, 2, 3		
	4.	Fuller	7/17/03	(598710)		D.	2, 1, 3, 5, 4		
	5.	Fuller	7/17/03	(598701)					
8.	1.	Perrine	10/27/99	(637096)		A.	3, 4, 5, 1, 2		8.__
	2.	Perrone	11/14/02	(767609)		B.	3, 2, 5, 4, 1		
	3.	Perrault	10/15/98	(629706)		C.	5, 3, 4, 1, 2		
	4.	Perrine	10/17/02	(373656)		D.	4, 5, 1, 2, 3		
	5.	Perine	10/17/01	(376356)					

KEY (CORRECT ANSWERS)

1. B
2. A
3. B
4. D
5. D
6. B
7. D
8. C

TEST 6

DIRECTIONS: Each question or incomplete statement is followed by several suggested answers or completions. Select the one that *BEST* answers the question or completes the statement. *PRINT THE LETTER OF THE CORRECT ANSWER IN THE SPACE AT THE RIGHT.*

1. Which one of the following *BEST* describes the usual arrangement of a tickler file?   1.____

   A. Alphabetical   B. Chronological
   C. Numerical   D. Geographical

2. Which one of the following is the *LEAST* desirable filing practice?   2.____

   A. Using staples to keep papers together
   B. Filing all material without regard to date
   C. Keeping a record of all materials removed from the files
   D. Writing filing instructions on each paper prior to filing

3. The one of the following records which it would be *MOST* advisable to keep in alphabetical order is a   3.____

   A. continuous listing of phone messages, including time and caller, for your supervisor
   B. listing of individuals currently employed by your agency in a particular title
   C. record of purchases paid for by the petty cash fund
   D. dated record of employees who have borrowed material from the files in your office

4. Tickler systems are used in many legal offices for scheduling and calendar control. Of the following, the *LEAST* common use of a tickler system is to   4.____

   A. keep papers filed in such a way that they may easily be retrieved
   B. arrange for the appearance of witnesses when they will be needed
   C. remind lawyers when certain papers are due
   D. arrange for the gathering of certain types of evidence

5. A type of file which permits the operator to remain seated while the file can be moved backward and forward as required is *BEST* termed a   5.____

   A. lateral file   B. movable file
   C. reciprocating file   D. rotary file

6. In which of the following cases would it be *MOST* desirable to have two cards for one individual in a single alphabetic file? The individual has   6.____

   A. a hyphenated surname
   B. two middle names
   C. a first name with an unusual spelling
   D. a compound first name

KEY (CORRECT ANSWERS)

1. B
2. B
3. B
4. A
5. C
6. A

———

Printed in the USA
CPSIA information can be obtained
at www.ICGtesting.com
LVHW080150131023
761005LV00011B/253